# ACHIEVEMENT
# MATTERS

# ACHIEVEMENT MATTERS

## GETTING YOUR CHILD THE BEST EDUCATION POSSIBLE

---

## HUGH B. PRICE

KENSINGTON PUBLISHING CORP.
http://www.kensingtonbooks.com

DAFINA BOOKS are published by

Kensington Publishing Corp.
850 Third Avenue
New York, NY 10022

All Kensington titles, imprints and distributed lines are available at special
quantity discounts for bulk purchases for sales promotion, premiums, fund-
raising, educational or institutional use.

Special book excerpts or customized printings can also be created to fit specific
needs. For details, write or phone the office of the Kensington Special Sales
Manager: Kensington Publishing Corp., 850 Third Avenue, New York, NY
10022. Attn. Special Sales Department. Phone: 1-800-221-2647.

Dafina and the Dafina logo Reg. U.S. Pat & TM Off.

ISBN 0-7582-0120-6

First Hardcover Printing: September 2002
First Trade Paperback Printing: July 2003
10  9  8  7  6  5  4  3  2  1

Printed in the United States of America

# CONTENTS

# ACKNOWLEDGMENTS

This is my first "real" book. In the past, the National Urban League has published compilations of my speeches and articles. But mustering the energy and self-confidence to write for a broad audience is a different enterprise altogether. This book bears the fingerprints of countless family members, friends, and colleagues who helped make it happen.

Let me begin with the folks who belong right up front in the "but for" category. But for my effervescent mother, Charlotte S. Price, and my late father, Dr. Kline A. Price Sr., who was an unflappable but firm role model, I would never have graced this earth and earned the chance to write this book. My brother, Dr. Kline A. Price Jr., is a highly respected physician whose inspiring response to every professional challenge I've ever faced is: "Go for it!"

My beloved wife, Marilyn L. Price, and our three precious daughters—Lauren A. Price, Janeen A. Price, and Traer E. Price—are the center of my universe, as is Traer's delightful husband, Steve Mitchell. I owe my career and whatever I've accomplished to them. Their love and the lives they've led helped spur me to write this book so I could share what I've learned as a husband and a father.

Thanks to my good friend Tom Dortch Jr., who is the national president of The 100 Black Men of America, I teamed up with an immensely talented writer, Carla Fine. We collaborated with ease, I'm convinced, because she's such a warm person who deeply understands why we must educate and develop America's children to their fullest potential. Leonor Ayala served with dedication and enthusiasm as our editorial assistant.

My savvy agents, Barbara Lowenstein and Madeline Morel, guided me through the process of prospecting for and selecting a publisher. The moment I met them, I could tell that Walter Zacharius, the founder and CEO of Kensington Books, and Karen Thomas, my talented and supportive executive editor at Kensington, shared my aspirations for this book and how to bring it to the broadest audience possible.

Much of what I have to say here derives from the work of the great Urban League movement, which I've been privileged to lead and to serve since July 1994. Rapidly approaching its second century of leadership and service, the Urban League is the oldest and largest community-based movement devoted to empowering African-Americans to enter the economic and social mainstream.

Many presidents of local Urban League affiliates caught the vision for our Campaign for African-American Achievement. I fondly recall stimulating conversations during the formative stages of the Achievement Campaign with legendary Urban League leaders such as Henry Thomas of Springfield, Massachusetts; T. Willard Fair of Miami; Eloise Gentry of Gary, Indiana; John Johnson of San Diego; James Buford of St. Louis; J. T. McLawhorn of Columbia, South Carolina; Dennis Walcott of New York City; Esther Bush of Pittsburgh; Don Bowen of Broward County, Florida; Maudine Cooper of Washington, D.C.; John Mack of Los Angeles; and the late Rev. William Clark of Kansas City. They are but a few of the incredibly dedicated and hardworking affiliate CEOs who give their all to the venerable Urban League movement and those we serve.

I owe an incalculable debt of gratitude to my gifted, hard-charging, and big-hearted colleagues at the National Urban League. It all starts with Milton Little, the League's executive vice president and chief operating officer, and with Dr. Velma Cobb, our director of education and youth development, who is the engine driving the Achievement Campaign. I'm also grateful to Velma's energetic and talented team, including Aaron Thomas, Renita Carter, Sherry Newton, Sandra Goodridge, Michelle Bullock, Darlene Burroughs, Jacqueline Mason, Nirvana Edwards, Katrina Mitchell, Tessie Spivey, and Vanessa Watson.

Other National Urban League colleagues who've played absolutely indispensable roles in the Achievement Campaign and its precursors include: Annelle Lewis, Mildred Love, Gena Davis-Watkins, Judith Little, Konrad Matthaei, Lee Daniels, Leslie Dunbar, Max Smith, Paul Wycisk, William Spriggs, Gasby Greely, and Phyllis Buford. Juliet Warner-Joseph, Joan Lucas, and Tyrone Phelps in the president's office at the League provide first-class, cheerful support, while laboring to keep me on track and on time. I'm indebted to countless other Urban Leaguers at the national and local levels over the years, but regrettably there isn't room here to mention everyone who has been helpful.

The Board of Trustees of the National Urban League has generously indulged and wholeheartedly supported my obsession with improving the academic achievement of our children. That starts with the trustees who have chaired the board on my watch—Reginald Brack, Jonathan Linen, and Kenneth Lewis. The senior vice-chairs of our board, Dr. Bernard Watson and Charles Collins, have been terrific friends and steadfast supporters as well.

Many other trustees have taken a keen interest in the League's Achievement Campaign, notably Eleanor Horne, the Rev. Franklyn Richardson, Stephanie Bell-Rose, William Lewis, Kevin Hooks, Ivan Seidenberg, Bill Stephany, Sean Barney, the Honorable Alexis Herman, Carolyn Wright Lewis, and Dr. Israel Tribble, the "godfather" of the National Achievers Society. Karla Ballard of the National Urban League Young Professionals offered many useful insights for this book and Pierre Bagley, the gifted filmmaker and founder of First Tuesday Productions, has brought the abstract idea of an Achievement Campaign vividly to life in his riveting videos. Dick Robinson, the CEO of Scholastic Inc. and his colleague Karen

Proctor have been enthusiastic and generous partners in the production and dissemination of the *Read and Rise* guide for parents and caregivers.

We were blessed at the League that many corporations and foundations cast their lot with our Achievement Campaign and the pilot initiatives that set the stage for it. I am deeply indebted to the following supporters: Monsanto Fund, Proctor & Gamble, Verizon Communications, State Farm Life Insurance Companies, Shell Oil Company, Met Life Foundation, Merrill Lynch, United Parcel Service Foundation, Major League Baseball, Sears Roebuck and Company, Borden's Inc., Coca-Cola Company, Exxon-Mobil, Duracell North Atlantic Group, Educational Testing Service, the Hartford, Freddie Mac Foundation, New York Stock Exchange, Compaq Computer Company, Gillette Company, Motorola, MTV Networks, Viacom International, American Airlines, Skyline Connections, Kraft Foods North America, McDonald's Corporation, MCI, Tommy Hilfiger, Amtrak, NIKE, Pfizer, the Gap Foundation, Marriott Corporation, Flagstar, Urban Cool Network, Darden Restaurants Foundation, and Jostens Renaissance.

Many foundations and agencies backed us along the way. The Lilly Endowment awarded us the largest foundation grant in the National Urban League's history. Other pivotal supporters include the Ford Foundation, John S. and James L. Knight Foundation, Pew Charitable Trusts, Robert Wood Johnson Foundation, U.S. Department of Education, Carnegie Corporation of New York, Annie E. Casey Foundation, Picower Foundation, Blanchette Hooker Rockefeller Fund, Starr Foundation, Hearst Foundation, Smith Richardson Foundation, Rockefeller Foundation, Joseph Drown Foundation, and Atlantic Philanthropic Services.

Over the years, I've drawn inspiration and intellectual sustenance from dozens of devoted national leaders, educators, school reformers, and youth development experts who I'm privileged to call authentic friends of young people—and of mine. I count the legendary school reformer, Dr. James P. Comer of the Yale University Child Study Center, as my principal mentor in these matters.

Other leaders with whom I've shared concerns and dreams,

ideas and schemes include: President George W. Bush; former President William J. Clinton; Secretary of State Colin L. Powell, who founded America's Promise; Marian Wright Edelman of the Children's Defense Fund; Professor Linda Darling-Hammond of Stanford University; Donald Stewart and Vinetta Jones of the College Board; Ernesto Cortes of the Industrial Areas Foundation; the Honorable James Hunt, former governor of North Carolina; U.S. Secretary of Education Rod Paige; the Honorable Richard Riley, former U.S. Secretary of Education; Ron Wolk of *Education Week;* Congressman Charles Rangel; Elaine Jones of the NAACP Legal Defense and Educational Fund; Raul Yzaguirre of the National Council of La Raza; Bob Schwartz of Achieve; Ed Joyner, Dr. Comer's long-standing colleague at Yale; and Jeff Howard of the Efficacy Institute.

The list of professional colleagues who've shaped my perspectives and priorities goes on: Marla Ucelli, Jamie Beck Jensen, Carol Mensah, Alberta Arthurs, and Judith Renyi of the Rockefeller Foundation; Willis Bright of the Lilly Endowment; Doug Besharov of the American Enterprise Institute; Professor Howard Gardner of Harvard Graduate School of Education; Professor Edmund Gordon of Columbia Teachers College and the College Board; Jan Kraemer of the Greater Kansas City Community Foundation and the Coalition of Community Foundations for Youth; Dan Donohue, the genius behind the National Guard Youth ChalleNGe Corps; the Rev. James Forbes of Riverside Church; Professor Christopher Edley Jr., of Harvard Law School; Professor John Simon of Yale Law School; Bishop John Hurst Adams of the Congress of National Black Churches; and Ronald Ross, superintendent of the Mount Vernon, New York, school system.

Others who have deeply influenced me include: Kati Haycock and Stephanie Robinson of the Education Trust; Dr. Nancy Cole, Kurt Landgraf, and Sharon Robinson of the Educational Testing Service; Bob Chase of the National Education Association; Sandra Feldman of the American Federation of Teachers; Gene Carter of the Association for Supervision and Curriculum Development; Rudy Crew of the Stupski Family Foundation; Gordon Ambach of the Council of Chief State School Officers; William Gray of the United Negro College Fund (UNCF); Dr. John Mason of the Monsanto Fund; Karen Pittman of the Forum for Youth Investment; Richard Murphy of the Center for Youth Development at the Academy for Educational Development; and the late Mitchell Sviridoff, another of my most valued mentors.

Thanks to their own values, many influential journalists have exhibited keen interest in the League's efforts to boost the academic achievement of black children. I refer particularly to Bill Raspberry of the *Washington Post*; Dewayne Wickham of *USA Today*; Bob Herbert of *The New York Times*, Angela King of *U.S. News & World Report*, and Paul Shepard of Associated Press. I'm indebted to Brian Lamb and his colleagues at C-SPAN for telecasting so many of my speeches and our policy forums on education reform.

Virginia Edwards, Sandra Reeves, Karla Reid, Caroline Hendrie, and Robert Johnston at *Education Week* have graciously covered the League's work and generously published numerous commentary articles of mine. Benjamin Todd Jealous, Frank Dexter Brown, and all the publishers affiliated with the National Newspaper Publishers Association have been right on the achievement page with us. Lon Walls and his conscientious team at Walls Communications have helped keep the League's achievement efforts and agenda in the public eye.

Closer to home, many treasured friends and neighbors have shaped my thinking over the years. They include Professor Hugh J. Scott of Hunter College; actor Ossie Davis; my fellow members of the Westchester Clubmen; schoolteacher and artist Patricia Richardson, who captured the essence of the Achievement Campaign in her glorious etching; Christopher Edley Sr., former head of UNCF; Dr. James Gaddy, former superintendent of the New Rochelle, New York, school system; and Margaret Young, the revered widow of Whitney M. Young, former head of the National Urban League, to name just a few.

Like everyone else, I can look back on teachers and coaches who genuinely believed in me, gently counseled me, and propelled me along the way toward whatever success I've achieved. The passage of time plus the onset of "old-timer's disease" (which jokesters say is the first stage of Alzheimer's disease) prevents me from recalling all their first names. Come to think of it, many teachers and principals back then didn't even have first names as far as their pupils were concerned.

In any event, I retain warm memories of Hilda Cobb, my wife's aunt who taught me at B. K. Bruce Elementary School in Washington, D.C.; her husband, Dr. Montague Cobb, the distinguished anatomist who started steering me toward his alma mater, Amherst College, as early as the sixth grade; both Mrs. Johnsons at Bruce; Mrs. Mills, a white teacher at newly integrated Taft Junior High School, who nonetheless pushed me hard academically; Mr. Brooks, my baseball coach in Taft's recreational programs, who filled my days with an after-school activity I never could get enough of; and last but by no means least, Ms. Anderson, my white homeroom teacher during those tense early years of integration at Coolidge High School, who spurred me to reach for the loftiest academic heights and never accepted halfhearted performance out of me.

Let me end these acknowledgments where everything begins— with the children, whose unshaped and thus unlimited potential inspires us all. I'm grateful to those bright young men I mentored as a law student—Butch Banks, Jimmy Stevens, Conley Monk, and their buddies—who showed me early in my career that mentoring pays handsome dividends for youngsters and for society. Nearly three decades later, the kids in "the Club," that inspiring program founded by the Westchester Clubmen, proved the same point even more convincingly.

The enthusiastic young people in the League's NULITES program (National Urban League Incentives to Excel and Succeed), along with the young scholars in our National Achievers Society, continue to inspire me. As do their parents, who are hell-bent on raising successful kids. Lastly, I thank those parents and young people who consented to be interviewed for this book, as well as the authors and task forces whose publications were such a valuable resource and a deep reservoir of relevant quotations that reminded everyone of their insightful points while helping me make mine.

These individuals and many others are my unofficial, behind-the-scenes coauthors who've earned a spot in the credit roll. It's abundantly clear by their words and deeds that they believe, as we Urban Leaguers do, that *Our Children = Our Destiny.*

# ACHIEVEMENT MATTERS

# INTRODUCTION

Education is the great equalizer in American society. It unlocks the doors to children's futures. It's the key to accessing opportunity and getting ahead in this country. Of course, education isn't a surefire guarantee of success in life. But statistics show beyond a shadow of a doubt that the better educated you are, the better off you'll be economically. And the more educated you are, the less likely you are to be unemployed. Getting a good education has always given young people a leg up on life. That was true in days gone by and it's truer today than ever before. The main reason for that is the way the U.S. labor market has changed over the years.

When I was growing up in the early 1950s, just about 80 percent of all the jobs in the U.S. economy were semiskilled or unskilled. That means most workers back then didn't require much in the way of formal education. Even if they never finished high school, they could easily earn enough, for instance, as factory workers to enjoy a decent standard of living, buy a home and a car, take an occasional vacation, and send their kids to college. The exact opposite is true today. Eighty-five percent of all jobs these days are skilled or professional. The bottom line is that you definitely need a solid education in order to succeed in the Information Age economy of the twenty-first century.

Yet the sad fact is that most African-American, Latino, and Native American children today aren't up to speed academically. They lag way behind where they should be—and where they could be—in terms of what they must know and be able to do in order to succeed in school and in life. Nor are they performing even close to on par with white and Asian-American youngsters.

Here's one barometer of how far behind the academic eight ball black children are. The National Assessment of Educational Progress (NAEP) is the nation's official report card on how America's children are doing in school. According to NAEP, in the year 2000, 63 percent of black youngsters read "below basic" in the fourth grade.

That's a couple of notches below grade level. In other words, two out of three black fourth-graders can barely read. They may recognize words in front of them, but they have little grasp of what they're reading. This dreadful statistic has barely changed in the past decade.

Latino and Native American fourth-graders fare slightly better, but even their performance is nothing to brag about. Among Latino fourth-graders, 58 percent scored "below basic" in 2000. The comparable figure for Native American kids was 57 percent. The picture for other youngsters is much brighter, however. Only 27 percent of white pupils in the fourth grade read "below basic." The ratio for Asian-American students was slightly lower—22 percent.

What's especially upsetting about the lousy performance of black children is the fact that Latino and Asian-American fourth-graders actually read better, even though English isn't the first language for many of them.

Youngsters who can barely read by the fourth grade face a steep uphill climb the rest of the way through school and later in life. They will struggle with the reading assignments in social studies, the writing assignments in English class, and the word problems in algebra. They probably won't be able to pass the tough exams that states are imposing for moving from grade to grade and for graduating from high school. Higher education will be off limits. The good jobs that provide for the good life will be out of reach for young people who aren't well prepared academically.

That is why every adult—every parent, every grandparent, every relative, and every foster parent—who is responsible for raising children in this day and age must be obsessed with making certain the young people they care about succeed in school. That they get the top-flight education they need and deserve. And that their children genuinely want to do well in school because they really do understand why achievement matters.

The days of letting our children view academic achievement as irrelevant, unimportant, "uncool," or "acting white" are long gone.

There is an African saying that's right on the mark: "Don't look where you have fallen, look where you slipped." We know that as parents, caregivers, and concerned members of the African-American community, we have much work to do to ensure that our children receive the education they deserve and acquire the skills they'll need to succeed as adults, as citizens, and as providers for themselves and their families.

Surveys show that African-American parents are deeply concerned about whether their children are getting a good education. They're also disturbed by a social and cultural climate that discourages young people from working hard to get good grades and excel in school.

So it's clear that parents care about education. The question posed by those dismal reading statistics is what are the practical things parents and caregivers can do to improve things for their children? That's exactly what this book intends to help you do.

Experts are fond of saying that parents are their children's first teachers. What do you suppose they mean by that? For me it means we must see to it that each and every child we're personally responsible for raising learns to read early on and acquires a love of learning. It means you must make certain that as your youngsters progress through school, they learn to read and write, calculate and compute, reason and solve problems, express themselves in mainstream language, navigate the Internet, and acquire the people skills and self-confidence to get along gracefully with others.

It means you should make certain your children can pass—and better yet, excel on—those exams given by states and school districts to determine whether students have the academic knowledge and skills to advance from grade to grade and eventually graduate from high school.

Remember—children spend most of their waking hours outside of school. As your children's first teacher, you set the tone at home.

To turn your youngsters on to school, you have to take the time and expend the effort to salute them for doing the right thing and publicly celebrate their academic success. You must remain steadfast and unwavering in order to provide a supportive and encouraging environment for the youngsters you are raising.

Above all, you must continue to urge your children to strive and persevere, even when others tell them they shouldn't excel in school. Keep watch on what they think of school. Don't let them be swayed by classmates who try to intimidate them emotionally or physically if they strive to do well. Whatever else you do, please don't let your children buy that anti-achievement baloney. It's a fool's errand and a road to nowhere.

Working with schools and community groups such as local Urban Leagues and Boys and Girls Clubs, parents and caregivers should pressure city officials, local foundations, and business leaders to offer sound programs after school that provide a safe haven, academic support, and constructive activities for youngsters while parents are still at work.

If we all do these things as parents and caregivers and as members of our community, we will close that embarrassing reading gap highlighted by NAEP. We'll equip even more of our youngsters to go on to colleges, universities, and trade schools. And we'll prepare them to earn a solid living or launch their own businesses.

By now you may be saying: "I hear you. Sign me up. Now what do I do next?"

What you should do is read the rest of this book. In it I lay out expert advice and real-world tips from everyday parents whose children have done very well in school. In the pages that follow, young people share their secrets to scholastic success. I also explain the highly successful programs that the Urban League and its partners in the Campaign for African-American Achievement have implemented to counteract that "anti-achievement" peer culture, spread the gospel that achievement matters, and convince our kids to take pride in their academic accomplishments.

The vast majority of black children attend public schools. So beyond doing what we must at home, improving public schools that perform miserably is the other key to boosting the achievement levels of children. In this book I explain how parents and community and business leaders have created a consumer demand for better schools and gotten results. In the twenty-first century, there must be zero tolerance for lousy schools.

If you accept inferior education for your children from this day forward, in effect you're signing a death warrant for their dreams. If you allow them to think academic achievement matters little, then odds are they'll amount to little.

But this doesn't have to be. Our children are every bit as eager and bright as other children. As their parents and first teachers, you are key to starting them out on the right track and making sure they stay on course.

With its inspiring stories, practical tips, and expert advice, *Achievement Matters* is your real-world guide to unlocking your children's potential and unleashing their dreams.

# CHAPTER ONE

## Taking Charge of Your Child's Education

My wife and I started our family in New Haven, Connecticut, where all three of our daughters were born and began school. In New Haven, parents in some of the public schools were pretty involved, although this was more an exception than the rule.

In 1968, we bought our first house on Ford Street in the predominantly black, working-class neighborhood of Newhallville. We lived right across the street from the brand new Martin Luther King Elementary School. As luck would have it, King was one of the first schools where the legendary educational reformer Dr. James Comer of the Yale University Child Study Center was launching his School Development Program (SDP). That year our eldest daughter entered kindergarten. It was just the second year of the SDP at King.

Dr. Comer really stressed parent involvement and building true partnerships and trust between the school staff and the parents. In fact, constructive and respectful collaboration was the key to his approach, a method which worked back then and which has proven its validity over time.

Parents at King really were into the school. They flocked to the meetings, meet-the-teacher nights, bake sales, and assemblies. That was easy for us, of course, because all we had to do was stroll across the street. It also helped that people didn't work such crazy hours in those days.

We knew our daughter's teachers and they knew us. More importantly, they knew that we cared about how she was doing academically. They also knew we were keeping an eagle eye on whether she was doing her schoolwork and whether they did their jobs as educators. Most other parents felt that way as well. The culture of the school reflected that enthusiastic involvement by parents and the trust we'd built up with the principal and teachers.

With the teachers' encouragement—and we would have done this whether they'd encouraged us or not—we kept a close eye on our daughter's report card and how she was doing, subject by subject. We made sure to check whether she was progressing properly, learning what she should, and performing at or above grade level.

Even when she came home with a really good report card, we would touch base with her teachers to confirm that she was doing nicely. We would ask whether there was anything they wanted us to work with her on or to do in order to ensure her academic success.

Now I need to confess that our daughters have always done well in school. Even so, that doesn't happen on automatic pilot. They worked very hard at it. So we were blessed that things tended to turn out well for them. Other than saying, as most youngsters do from time to time, that school was *boring,* they always took academic achievement seriously.

So to be perfectly truthful about it, our daughters didn't present us, or their teachers, with some of the very stiff challenges that other youngsters pose. Yet the other parents at King, most of whom were working people instead of professionals and some of whom were on welfare, were every bit as involved in King, equally dedicated, and just as vigilant as we were. Their commitment to King really showed in the positive environment at the school and, above all, in the impressive scholastic gains posted by the students.

Other schools in the city struggled to get parents to care. Attendance at meet-the-teacher nights was sparse. Parents didn't feel all that welcome in their school. Their lack of engagement showed in their academic results. What was it that set King apart from other inner-city schools in New Haven? Purely and simply, it was parental involvement.

King started out as one of the weakest schools in the district academically. But using Dr. Comer's approach—with its emphasis on active and authentic parent engagement—King steadily climbed to near the top of the academic ratings in the school district.

In July 1978, we moved south, from New Haven to New Rochelle, New York. New Rochelle is situated in Westchester County, which is predominantly middle class and heavily upper middle class. The difference between the two towns in terms of parent involvement was eye-opening. The level of involvement that we'd experienced even at King paled by comparison with the way parents monitor schools in New Rochelle.

We moved to New Rochelle because I took a job with *The New York Times*. Three weeks later, yes, three weeks later, we went out on strike at the *Times*. I was out of work and off a payroll for the first time in my life. Mind you, my wife hadn't started working, so this really was belt-tightening time when it came to family income.

Initially I figured the strike wouldn't last more than a week or two. So I took advantage of the lull in the employment action by sleeping late, watching New York Yankee baseball games, and puttering around the house. Meanwhile our eldest daughter entered the ninth grade, and the younger two enrolled in elementary school.

Since we had enrolled our children in a new school system, I decided to see how it worked first chance I got. Several weeks after school opened, I ventured out to meet-the-teacher night at the junior high school. I was dumbfounded and dazzled by the turnout. So many parents were there that night that the school had to hire off-duty policemen to direct the traffic. Each classroom I visited averaged one parent—and often two—per pupil. Sometimes it was standing room only.

I'll never forget a couple of encounters between my daughter's ninth-grade math teacher and some parents, which showed how closely New Rochelle parents were on the case. The teacher, who was in a grouchy mood, opened the session by explaining how disappointed she was that the youngsters weren't doing well in her class. In response, one parent raised her hand and then announced that her son, who actually was an eighth-grader, attended this class because he was very bright and that she, the mother, possessed a doctorate degree in math. The youngster's mother stated firmly that if her son wasn't performing well, it was the teacher's fault and that the teacher had better check herself out.

Her blunt comment rattled the teacher momentarily, but she recovered. She went on a few moments later to note how many pupils had gotten the wrong answer on a math problem that very day that they should easily have been able to handle. The teacher wrote out the problem on the blackboard and worked through to the answer. Within an instant, another parent in the back of the room raised his hand. He told the teacher that if she figured out the problem over again and with care, she would discover that she'd arrived at the wrong answer. The silence in the classroom was deafening.

This encounter shows how closely these parents monitored their children's academic performance, their schools, and even their teachers. They turned out in huge numbers to make certain that both the educators and their own children knew that what was happening in school was critically important to them and that they had every intention of staying right on the case.

Now I'm not naive. I don't expect every parent to be able to figure out the correct answer to that math problem. I sure couldn't have. But by virtue of their determined presence and by quizzing the teachers closely on how their youngsters were doing academically, the parents were keeping their children and the teachers on their toes. So I know firsthand from our own daughters' positive academic experience in school that parental vigilance definitely pays off.

Youngsters whose parents aren't active can be overlooked in the shuffle. That's why parents must make their presence felt, so the schools don't slack off or shower attention only on the children of the squeaky wheels. In addition, the children will get the message that the right to a quality education is something worth fighting for. As Temple University pyschology professor Laurence Steinberg writes in his book *Beyond the Classroom:* "If we want our children and teenagers to value education and strive for achievement, adults must behave as if doing well in school is more important than any other activity in which young people are involved."

Parental involvement is key to academic success. In the remainder of this chapter, I'll present specific ways to make sure your children are provided with the fundamental academic knowledge and practical skills they'll need to succeed in a complex and competitive world.

## YEARS OF PROMISE

Will Rogers, the wise humorist, once said: "Things will get better despite our efforts to improve them." For the sake of our children, we must do better than that.

According to the Carnegie Task Force on Learning in the Primary Grades, the years from three to ten are a crucial age span in a young person's life. This is when a firm foundation for healthy development and lifelong learning is put into place. For most children, the long-term success of their learning and development depends to a great extent on what happens to them during these formative years of promise.

The importance of success in school during this time is profound. A child's basic sense of worth depends heavily on the ability to achieve in school. If the adults who matter in a child's life expect little and provide scant support, then defeatism quickly sets in. That alienates them from education and undermines their desire to do well academically for years to come.

Jeff Howard, founder of the Efficacy Institute, cites something called "attribution theory" to explain poor academic performance. Children whose teachers and, yes, even whose parents don't expect them to do well in school then don't even strive to do well. In these youngsters' minds, if they don't try to excel, they can't be branded as failures because they never tried in the first place. So low expectations fuel defeatism and perpetuate a vicious cycle of school failure.

As their children's first teachers, parents must nip defeatism in the bud by setting high standards for their youngsters and regularly telling their children they have every confidence they can meet them. Parents should convey those high expectations to their teachers so the schools aren't allowed to undermine the kids' self-confidence or scholastic performance.

All children are born ready and eager to learn. Visit any nursery school or Head Start program or kindergarten class. You can feel the excitement in the air as these children respond enthusiastically to new activities and challenges. See the inquisitiveness in their eyes, the smile on their faces, the enthusiasm of their responses to their teacher's attention.

If youngsters come out of the womb this way, then why in the world do so many bright and beautiful children lose their God-given curiosity and eagerness as they move through school? Why do such an alarmingly high percentage of minority and poor children perform so poorly in school? To get even more basic, why is it that two-thirds of African-American fourth-graders can barely read, year after year after year?

The answer is well documented by Jonathan Kozol, author of *Savage Inequalties,* and by scores of impartial studies. As things now stand, the deck all-too-often is unfairly stacked against poor and minority children. The preschool programs they start out in should be stronger. The schools they attend must get better. And to be frank about it, they need more support, guidance, and encouragement at home from day one.

As loving parents and caregivers, you mustn't allow your children to receive a slipshod education. There definitely are concrete things you can do to make a difference. Here's what we know works:

• *At Home.* Children whose parents are involved in their education and create a home environment that encourages learning earn higher grades than children whose parents aren't involved.

• *In the Community.* Youngsters from communities that offer after-school programs emphasizing learning and practical help for parents to promote academic achievement and healthy child development do better in school than children whose communities don't support them this way.

• *In Preschool Programs.* Children who are fortunate enough to attend a high-quality preschool or child care program and who enter grade school solidly prepared are more likely to do well academically than children whose preschool preparation is weak.

• *In Elementary Schools.* Children who attend an elementary school that sets high standards and does whatever is necessary to see that children meet them are more prone to leave the fourth grade proficient in reading, writing, math, and science than youngsters attending a school that expects little of them.

"You have to expect that children will do well and then do whatever you can to make them learn," says Velma Cobb, my colleague at the National Urban League who directs the Campaign for African-American Achievement. "Even though many parents believe that the school system is not set up to prepare their children for academic success, there's enough research and pockets of successful schools to show that we can educate our children well if we are committed to these kids come hell or high water."

It sounds trite, but it's so true that I'll repeat it. Parents and caregivers are children's first teachers. You must become involved—early and actively—in instilling a love and respect for learning in your sons and daughters. The key is to get all children on the educational fast track right from the start as early as possible so that school becomes a voyage of discovery they look forward to instead of a source of failure they shun.

## THE PREPARATION GAP

We hear lots of anxious talk these days about achievement gaps. The media moans about it. Organizations like the National Urban

League, which I head, agonize over it. Pundits complain and pontif-
icate about it. Public school educators under siege try to duck responsibility by making excuses for it.

When you think about it, there actually are several achievement
gaps. There's the gap between how American children in general
and black youngsters in particular stack up against children in the
rest of the world. Then there's the disturbing fact that when you
compare what youngsters know and can do, a pupil who earns an
A in an inner-city school knows about as much in a given subject as
a suburbanite who earns a C. Put another way, black and Latino
twelfth-graders in urban schools stack up about equally with white
suburbanites in the eighth grade.

The achievement gap isn't confined to inner-city and rural schools.
Middle-class black kids in integrated suburban schools generally
lag behind their white and Asian-American classmates.

So any way you measure it or however you explain it, these
achievement gaps along ethnic and economic lines are distressing.
Society should summon the will and allocate the resources to close
these gaps. It's a moral and economic imperative, in my opinion.

There's another way of looking at the achievement gap that
doesn't get nearly as much attention. But I happen to think that
closing this one is more urgent for parents, communities, and society at large. It's what I'd call *The Preparation Gap*.

You're probably wondering what I mean by *The Preparation
Gap*. It's the gap between what poor and minority children know
vs. what they need to know in order to meet state academic standards, move from one grade to the next, and eventually graduate
from high school. There's also that gap between what they can do
and what they must be able to do in order to land good jobs and get
into college and trade schools. These are the gaps that I believe
must be closed ASAP. Why? Because if we don't, the children won't
have the knowledge and skills they need to become self-reliant
adults and informed citizens.

As the late President Richard Nixon once said, let me make one
thing perfectly clear. I am as determined as the next person to close
those achievement gaps that divide ethnic and socioeconomic groups.

But the vastly more urgent task in my view is to eliminate *The Preparation Gap*. Until *we* do, low achievers will stay stuck behind the eight ball, woefully unqualified for higher education and the increasingly demanding world of work.

The seeds of *The Preparation Gap* are planted early in a child's life, often unintentionally or usually without parents even noticing what's happening. It starts with preschool. Many child care providers and day care centers that parents send their preschoolers to offer only custodial care and recreation. Assuming they even have one, their formal "curriculum" devoted to preparing youngsters properly for reading may be weak or improvised. It often isn't based on the best available research and practice about preparing preschoolers to become good readers and eager learners.

According to the Carnegie Corporation, the vast majority of early child care and education programs fail to meet accepted standards of quality. As a result, as many as one-third of American children enter kindergarten already behind their age group whose preschool experience was more solid. As early as kindergarten, black and Hispanic pupils already trail behind white and Asian-American kindergarteners on exams that gauge general knowledge and early reading and math skills. So right off the bat, many minority children require extra help in order to catch up and keep up with their peers.

*The Preparation Gap* persists and even widens as they move through elementary school. These years are a defining experience for children that will heavily shape their lives all the way through adolescence and beyond.

For most schoolchildren, the early elementary grades are when the so-called "ability sorting" really begins. Children are steered onto academic paths that they'll pretty much follow the rest of the way through school. That's fine if your child lands on a path headed toward high academic standards. But if the route is littered with low expectations, your child could be headed for frustration, academic failure, and trouble.

Parents who aren't paying close attention often find out too late that their kids lose interest in learning sometime around the third grade or so and their grades fall off the cliff. Educators say this is especially a problem among black boys. The damage often can't be undone, and when it can be, it takes years of extra instruction and tutoring. This dashes the children's dreams by undermining their interest in school and destroying their confidence that they'll ever become achievers. So they cease trying and the cycle of academic failure spins on the rest of the way through school until they dial out completely or actually drop out.

It doesn't get any easier to close *The Preparation Gap* when students move on to middle school. Just think about it. Youngsters who can barely read won't be able to handle the word problems in algebra or read the instructions for science experiments, much less complete the reading assignments in social studies. If they cannot read, writing probably will be a struggle as well. So English class will be a severe challenge for weak students.

The problems that surface in elementary school don't disappear in high school either. In fact, as youngsters approach the end of adolescence, the stakes from *The Preparation Gap* get much higher. They are held back in grade and sent off to summer school. They fail the tougher exams imposed by states and school districts and cannot graduate from high school. They do miserably on college entrance exams and cannot qualify for admission. They score poorly on tests required by employers and cannot land those good-paying skilled and professional positions that comprise 85 percent of all the jobs available. That frustrates job applicants and employers alike. When you add it all up, inferior education leads to economic apartheid.

What explains these gaps that seldom go away? One expert, Stephanie Bell-Rose, president of the Goldman Sachs Foundation, believes that what teachers teach and how well they teach it is perhaps the most important variable affecting how youngsters perform. "Unfortunately, black students generally attend schools with fewer resources, larger class sizes, and less-qualified teachers," she concludes.

Another culprit is low expectations. According to a National Urban League survey conducted in 2001 of black Americans under the age of 35, 51 percent believed that public school teachers had a lower expectation for black student performance than for white students.

You can be sure students notice it when teachers don't think they amount to much academically. "Sometimes I think my teacher doesn't call on me because he just assumes I don't know the answer," says Omar, a fifth-grader from Chicago. "Some teachers stereotype African-American males. It's like the movie *Finding Forrester,* where they think you're up to no good because you're black and live in the projects. But racial profiling just encourages me to do better. I want to show them they're wrong and it makes me want to work harder."

To help your children reach their highest potential, parents should familiarize themselves with the academic standards they're expected to meet and when the schools give those critically important tests that assess whether they do.

Parents don't necessarily have to figure this out by themselves. The New York Urban League, for instance, operates its Standard Keepers Program that teaches parents about the academic standards and exams in the New York City schools. The program informs them about the specific academic standards their children must meet from grades three through eight, and explains assorted tests their children must take to see if they measure up to these standards.

"In order to know if your children are being adequately prepared to meet the academic requirements in their grade level, parents have to know what their children are supposed to learn," says LaVerne Bloomfield-Jiles, director of Standard Keepers, which is part of the national Campaign for African-American Achievement. "Parents go from being passive to active participants in their children's education because now they understand how their children should perform on a grade-by-grade basis. They can begin to gauge their children's performance on an objective basis and not have to rely solely on a teacher's evaluation."

Standard Keepers encourages parents and caretakers to establish and build relationships with their children's teachers. Parents learn how to make sense of their child's report card. Plus they are prepped on the types of questions they should ask at conferences with their child's teacher.

"Let's say a father doesn't know what to ask about his daughter's performance in her third-grade math class," Ms. Bloomfield-Jiles explains. "He might not even know the type of math she's being taught. We prepare a list of questions for the father so he can get a better idea of what his daughter should be studying and the tests she is required to pass. He can then monitor his daughter's progress himself and make sure she is keeping up with the rest of her class.

"We believe strongly that parental participation is the key to a child's success. We're not comparing student to student, but how each individual child is able to meet the expected standard in every grade and level. By preparing parents to be the Keepers of the Standards for their children, we are helping to close the achievement gap by making parents—not a large and impersonal school system—to be the ultimate caretakers of their child's education."

Standard Keepers helps parents participate knowledgeably in their youngster's education. I would urge parents and caregivers to find out whether there's a program like this in your neighborhood. If there isn't, ask a community-based agency or even your church to start up one. Or you could ask the school principals to provide this kind of information. If they care at all about kids, they'll probably be pleasantly surprised to get a request like this and probably will be pleased to help.

## YOU DEFINITELY CAN MAKE A DIFFERENCE

When it comes to literacy, the adults who rear children make a huge difference. But it doesn't come easy and cannot be done on cruise control. You must be willing after a hard day's work to tuck your child in after supper and read to her until she falls asleep. And when she's older, have her read to you before you doze off. Even if you can't help them with homework, you have to keep a close enough eye on them to know whether they're doing it themselves. No matter how much they protest, you have to limit how much television they watch. You have to get up and out on a Saturday morning to take your son to a museum or the library. I don't care how fatigued you are from work, you have to find the time and energy to attend parent-teacher conferences at school.

Research shows that parents still matter the most. In examining the lessons from the fourth-grade test results in 2000, the authors of the NAEP report found that students who talk about their schoolwork with their parents and live in a home where reading materials are widely available actually read on a higher level than other children.

"Parents are the most important teachers," says Stephanie Akpa, 17, co-president of the 21st Century Youth Leadership Team of the San Diego Urban League. "My advice to younger kids is to make sure that someone cares about you—a parent, a teacher, a relative, a mentor—and don't be afraid to ask them for help.

"On a certain level, I feel I'm getting good grades not only for myself but also for other students who know they can do the same," Stephanie explains. "It's important that African-American young people set good examples and show that we can achieve and do well. Our team proves that we can be achievers and we're backing it up by our actions. The more we do, the more we break the negative stereotypes about black youth. We are the future and must always remember that we should serve as mentors to others."

The active involvement of parents is the first step in creating a level educational playing field. Parental involvement in a school can help turn it from a failure to a center of excellence. They can influence the choice of the principal, the type of curricula, the quality of teaching, and the expectations of teachers, along with the provisions for security and safety in the classrooms.

The plain fact is that the academic achievement level of young people is in direct proportion to the caliber and consistency of support adults provide for them. According to a study published in the

*American Educational Research Journal,* parental involvement has been shown to influence children's achievement in language and mathematics, their academic persistence, their behavior problems, and whether or not they remain in school or drop out.

"My parents set up a structure," says Shawn M. Barney, a 26-year-old partner in a wireless technology company and a member of the League's Board of Trustees. "Every morning my father took me to school. I grew up in New Orleans and went to public school through the eighth grade, then to an all-male, all-black high school. Driving to school with my dad was our private time together and I really treasured it. We would discuss anything and everything as we shared our McDonald's breakfast in the car. It was spending time together on a consistent basis, and I knew I could always count on it. Now I have a friend who walks his 8-year-old daughter to school every morning, and I plan to do the same thing when I have my own children.

"My parents were very active in my education—they went to PTA meetings and made it a point to meet all my teachers. They instilled an independence in me and the goal of being successful in whatever I chose to do in my life. I understood that doing well in school was important because the A's I got would be further communicated down the road and would have consequences as a result. I also felt my mother and father really cared about me and were on my side. I knew that if something was wrong, they would work with me to try to fix it. It was as if I had constant backup, which gave me a lot of confidence and self-esteem."

Even so, parents also have to be backed up by the educational and political system: it won't work if you're out there all alone. For example, a *Chicago Tribune* survey found that of the city's 550 public schools, only 24 had levels of high parental involvement. As a result, Chicago Mayor Richard Daley held a series of citywide assemblies to arm adults with the skills and knowledge to help their children with schoolwork and boost parental involvement in order to improve children's performance in the classroom.

The assemblies were open to all adults with children in public, private, or parochial schools. The gatherings featured workshops on topics ranging from "Raising a Reader" and "Working with Your Child's Teacher to Improve Performance," to "The Effects of Health and Nutrition on Your Child's Learning." The workshops provided information about services and programs readily available for adults who are raising children.

Another shining example are the public schools of Mount Vernon, a Westchester County suburb just north of New York City. The pupils in the failing school system were predominately black and poor. Ronald O. Ross, a former teacher and principal, was brought in to turn the school system around and indeed he did. Within two years, the district boasted three of the most improved schools in the state for fourth-grade reading test scores. Several of the district's elementary schools had more than doubled the percentage of students passing the tests since 1999, the first year they were given. Mount Vernon soared from roughly 35 percent of the fourth-graders passing the state literacy arts exam in 1999, to nearly 75 percent by 2001.

Teachers and principals were involved in Mount Vernon's turnaround, but so were parents. After the first grade, all students had to write in a journal each night when they got home. In addition, parents had to sign forms confirming that their child read for thirty minutes every night. This shows again that for academically successful children, education doesn't stop when the school bell rings.

Another impressive parental involvement program is The Right Question Project in Cambridge, Massachusetts. Parents in the Boston area who get hold of computers can go online at www.rightquestion.org and find out specific information about their child's school.

Parental interest and involvement reinforce the natural inclination of children to strive to do their best. Lousy schools with apathetic and alienated pupils can improve only if the adults in their lives mobilize to make it happen and refuse to accept any excuses for failure.

A third-grader from Ft. Lauderdale named Cheryl cut right to the chase when she said: "It's important for parents to give you support and motivation. That way you don't feel alone."

Here are some basic ways you can help your children develop a thirst for learning and acquire the skills they'll need to do well in school.

1. Get an early start on making sure your children become good readers by reading to them from the time they are toddlers and having them read to you as soon as they're able. In Chapter 3, "Reading," I lay out some practical tips on how to do this.

2. Use everyday occurrences, such as cooking and family trips, as ways of helping youngsters practice doing math and learning to look up things in books.

3. Be sure they read for fun because that builds a love of learning and discovery through reading, and besides, practice makes proficient readers.

4. Help them turn their favorite hobbies into enjoyable learning experiences that enable them to practice skills they are taught in school.

5. Visit the school on parent-teacher nights and in-between if necessary, so both the teachers and your child know that you mean business when it comes to your children getting a good education.

6. Establish appropriate routines at home, like creating quiet time for homework and recreational reading, and limiting the amount of television they can watch.

7. Visit libraries, bookstores, and book fairs with your children so they can see that reading is important to you and that it should be to them.

I would characterize these as constructive activities that help youngsters acquire an appetitite for learning and a positive attitude toward school. I hate to say it, but parents must also keep an eagle eye out for any sign of academic slippage by their children or slipshod education by the school. Since it's black, Latino, and Native American youngsters who usually lag way behind, their parents especially must stay on the lookout against their children losing ground. Here are some ways to keep watch:

1. Given the tendency of black youngsters to slip backward around the third or fourth grade, you should be especially alert for any backsliding in these grades even if they did well in the early years.

2. Monitor each report card and make sure your child is performing at grade level or better. Don't just accept the teacher's word for it. Ask to see the data and test scores. Even if they're performing on grade, ask the teacher how both of you can help them do even better. If they are slipping behind, develop a game plan in partnership with the teacher to get them up to speed.

3. Talk frequently with your children about what's happening in class. Ask to see any notices from the teacher, guidance counselor, or principal. Look for signs that they are extremely bored, disengaged, dropping out, or withdrawn from school. Seek counseling to get them back on track before it's too late.

4. Challenge any suggestions by the schools to place your child in special education. Insist on receiving a second opinion about whether the placement really is necessary. Since the pattern of wrongful and unneeded assignment to the purgatory of special ed is so widespread and pernicious, seek expert second opinions before consenting.

5. Work closely with teachers to ensure that early warning systems are in place and make certain that activities and supervision outside of school are fully in synch with what happens inside the classroom.

6. Keep your kids from falling under the influence of friends and classmates who say achievement isn't important. Cheer them on at home, show up when they're involved in a school

event, and join with other parents, school officials, and community groups like the local Urban League in saluting them for striving to excel in school.

7. If doing these kinds of things is a struggle for you, admit it for the sake of your children and ask a relative, a friend, or a pastor for help in keeping close tabs on how your youngsters are doing and in working with the school to implement an action plan for improvement.

## WATCH OUT ESPECIALLY FOR SPECIAL ED

For far too many children, referral to special education is a one-way ticket to failure. Special ed often derails students from a regular education. I'm talking about students who, if they were given intensive instruction, would be capable of doing quite well in mainstream classes alongside other children who haven't been labeled or stigmatized. In some big-city school systems, fewer than 5 percent of special ed children ever escape or, as bureaucrats say, are "decertified."

African-American parents must be wary because racial discrimination is rampant in special ed, despite its supposedly noble intentions. According to an alarming study by the Civil Rights Project at Harvard University, black students were three times more likely than their white classmates to be identified as mentally retarded; almost twice as likely to be identified as emotionally disturbed; and 1.3 times as likely to be identified with a specific learning disability. What's even more astonishing, the Harvard researchers reported that black boys living in wealthier communities with strong, integrated schools were more prone to be sent to special classes than black students attending predominantly black schools in low-income neighborhoods.

Children who are diagnosed with these "problems" can be forced to attend special education classes where progress is slow and properly trained teachers are scarce. Youngsters who land in special ed tend to get in more trouble with the law. Many minority children who are sent to special education never return to regular classes. Some school systems have even been accused of sticking weak students in special ed, where their test scores aren't pooled with the regular pupils, so the school will rank higher based on its overall test scores.

Now I'm not saying that there's never a need for special education. Clearly some children suffer emotional and physical handicaps that seriously impede their ability to learn in a traditional classroom, where instruction moves at a pace prescribed by state academic standards and exams.

But parents must be vigilant about making sure that their child actually needs to be in special education classes before they agree to it. Oftentimes, teachers will place students there because they're doing poorly or because they pose behavioral problems. In truth, these kids may be plenty bright but hopelessly bored, hyperactive, and hard to manage. Inexperienced or culturally insensitive teachers may be ill-equipped to capture their attention and gain their confidence. Special education programs are often used as a dumping ground for lazy or burned-out teachers who don't want to make the effort to help children who may be a challenge to teach.

Labels stick. Original labels can stick the longest and do lasting harm. A child classified as "different," who goes to classes apart from other children or travels to another school, may start doubting his or her own academic abilities. It's worth remembering that faulty diagnosis also endangered the future of many noted Americans who were labeled dyslexic and written off early on by their teachers. The celebrated filmmaker George Lucas comes quickly to mind.

"I was told that special ed was the only way to help my 6-year-old granddaughter," says Brenda, a college professor from Houston. "Her teacher and the school's guidance counselor told me that she was a 'slow learner' and would do better in a different kind of setting. But do I really want my granddaughter, who's very timid and small for her age, in a classroom with kids who are continually acting up? How will she learn if she's distracted and maybe even afraid?"

I was horrified by what Theresa Sanders, head of the Urban League of Long Island, told me almost happened to her daughter. She's a very strong student, so one day Ms. Sanders paid a visit to the guidance counselor to find out how to get her into Advanced Placement courses. The counselor said he wasn't equipped to do that, nor did he so much as offer to find out how and get back to her. However, he did say he had all the forms handy in case she wanted to place her daughter in special education. Of course, this savvy mother told the useless counselor what he could do with his forms.

All children enter school at the same grade level. Once enrolled, a child can be tracked—as early as first grade—into an honors/advanced/gifted program, a regular class, or a special education section. In Chapter 5, "Navigating the School System," I will go into more detail about what you can do to navigate your way through the school system so your child isn't derailed academically by being steered down the wrong track.

What happened to Theresa Sanders and her daughter is downright scandalous. Nor is hers an isolated story. It illustrates the pervasive discrimination in special education that parents constantly must guard against.

## COLLEGE LESSONS ABOUT ACADEMIC SUCCESS

College is another place to look for helpful lessons about how to improve the achievement levels of youngsters in elementary and secondary school. There are programs in higher education I've heard about that do a terrific job of boosting the scholastic performance of minority students. Even though the students who participate obviously are older, these programs have much to say to parents and caregivers whatever their child's age.

A fine example is the Meyerhoff Scholars program at the University of Maryland/Baltimore County. It prepares talented African-American students for research careers in science and engineering. The program was created in 1988 by Dr. Freeman Hrabrowski, a distinguished African-American mathematician and scientist who is president of the university. He was disturbed by the shortage of blacks in these fields and determined to do something about it at his campus. More than 100 Meyerhoff Scholars have already graduated, and almost all of them are enrolled in graduate and professional programs in the sciences and medicine. The program originally focused on males, but now it includes female students.

Dr. Hrabowski coauthored a book about the program. It's entitled *Beating the Odds: Raising Academically Successful African American Males.* He also is coauthoring a sequel on raising academically successful young women. The original book describes how the families of the Meyerhoff Scholars went about rearing academically successful sons who scored among the top 2 percent of black males in terms of SAT scores and grades. One key is that these parents became quite assertive, even forceful, whenever they spotted signs that:

1. The schools had low expectations for their sons.
2. Their sons seemed to be the victims of some type of discrimination at school.
3. Their children had problems at school.

"The critical importance of parental contact and involvement in the school to academic success cannot be overstated," the authors write. "Many social science research studies have linked greater levels of parental involvement in education with higher educational achievement. Here we find that for African-American males in particular, parents put forth extreme efforts to help ensure that their sons successfully overcame the barriers and temptations that have tragically undermined and derailed the academic focus of so many other capable black youth."

Young men who became Meyerhoff Scholars attribute their academic success to several factors, including positive neighborhood and school environments, self-esteem, and religious beliefs. Yet the reason they cited most frequently by far is parental support and involvement in their schooling. These sons tell of parents who were constantly in contact with their classroom teachers; attended parent-teacher conferences on a regular basis; visited their classrooms to observe how they were being taught; made sure they were appropriately placed in academically challenging classes and programs; kept an open line of communication with their guidance counselor and school principal; and participated in the PTA and school volunteer work.

For their part, the parents emphasize the critical importance of holding high expectations for their children. They constantly pushed their sons to achieve, reminding them over and over that they could excel in school. If their sons fell back for any reason, they had to explain what was wrong and why they were not getting the best grades. When they did well in school, their parents showered praise on them. They also expected their youngster's social behavior to be exemplary. These lessons apply equally to boys and girls.

The bottom line is that these determined adults value the importance of high-quality education for their kids and work tirelessly to make sure they receive the best preparation possible. Every adult who is raising a child should have the same mind-set.

Ron is a U.S. customs agent in Detroit who is the father of two young sons and a daughter. "Parents have to stay up to date on what's going on in their children's lives," he says. "All children are different from each other and parents must value each as distinct individuals. You have to hear what they're saying to you and try to be objective and not judge them. I grew up without a father, and I vowed that when I had children, I would always be there for them. I'm proud to say that I am convinced that my daughter and sons' schoolwork reflects the constant attention and presence of my wife and myself."

"African Americans need as much education as possible in order to help others," the authors of *Beating the Odds* write. "If blacks achieve more academically, they will be able to combat the insidious message that achievement in school is not to be valued."

Experts remind us that education isn't confined to the classroom. Nor does it end when school adjourns every June or when youngsters graduate. According to Emma M. Talbott, author of *The*

*Joy and Challenge of Raising African American Children,* learning
is ongoing and lifelong. In her book, she offers may practical ideas
for fostering educational success through family togetherness and
discovery. Admittedly some activities take money, but that isn't true
of all of them. Imagination is the only limit on the ways you and
your child can learn together. Here are some of Ms. Talbott's effective ideas, along with several more of mine:

1. Explore African-American culture and learn about other
   ethnic groups as well.
2. Visit historic places, libraries, museums, concerts, and plays.
3. Work to improve your children's communication skills and
   make sure they have full command of standard English regardless of the slang they may use among friends.
4. Engage in dialogue with your children and tell them stories
   of your childhood.
5. Be selective about what your children watch on television.
6. Teach them the games you played back when you were
   growing up.
7. Play educational games with them.
8. Encourage your children to have hobbies that promote
   learning and discovery, like collecting rocks or stamps.
9. Purchase a computer for your home and invest in an ency-
   clopedia—in print or online.
10. Subscribe to a reputable newspaper and have your child
    read it.
11. Encourage your children to write by keeping a diary or
    journal.

Candace Smith is a successful young attorney with a large law
firm in Atlanta and a member of the National Urban League's
Board of Trustees. A graduate of Brown University and Harvard
Law School, Candace says that the more support she received, the
better she did in school.

"My parents and grandmother were always asking me about my
studies and took a great interest in my schoolwork," she says. "It's

so important to be encouraged and feel that your achievements are acknowledged and rewarded. Children feel more confident and self-assured knowing that there are adults who care about and support them. Every parent has the tools to reinforce academic achievement by showing enthusiasm and being actively engaged in their children's education."

## EQUALITY BEGINS WITH EDUCATION

African Americans have always valued education and viewed it as the surest route to success. "[I]n this society, education opens the door to success," writes sociology professor Walter R. Allen in *The State of Black America 2001,* a publication of the National Urban League. "Because talent is significantly equated with high educational performance and attainment, the cherished belief that even the poorest American can, with hard work and determination, achieve greatness is a linchpin of the belief that education is the foundation of democracy."

Academic failure simply isn't an option in the Information Age economy of the twenty-first century. It's essential to economic self-sufficiency and effective citizenship in the twenty-first century. Parents must begin to think—and participate—"outside of the box." As your children's first teacher, you owe it to them to take charge of their learning and development at home and also get involved at the community level and in the political process.

Attend school board meetings and keep the members' feet to the fire about focusing on the best interests of your child and all of the children. Pressure them to boost student achievement by improving teaching and learning inside the classroom instead of cracking down mercilessly on kids through measures like ending social promotion and mandating summer school. Those are Band-Aid measures, bred of panic and political sloganeering, that ignore a truism that's both obvious and proven by research: The caliber of classroom instruction must be raised in order for student performance to rise.

To paraphrase Peter Finch's cry of frustration in that celebrated film *Network,* "We're mad as hell and we're not going to take it anymore." Tell your local school board in no uncertain terms that you have zero tolerance for lousy schools—and so must they. If your child's school performs miserably year after year, get impatient. Get angry. Get involved. Insist on answers, and if none are forthcoming, demand alternatives. Join forces with other parents, community groups, and business leaders to pressure politicians at the local, state, and federal levels for wise policies and adequate funding for the schools.

Breadwinners work hard these days providing for their families. In fact, some studies show that on average we toil the equivalent of one month longer than our parents did. So it's no wonder that we often have little energy left when we get home. If the traditional methods of getting involved are too taxing for you, here's another approach worth trying. What about forming a support group made up of parents and caregivers who face similar pressures. Members could alternate going to key meetings of the school board and at school, and later on brief one another on important developments, key policy debates, and upcoming decisions where parents' voices should be heard.

The clock is ticking. America's heavy-duty reliance on well-educated workers will never reverse course. That's why we no longer have time *not* to have time for our children. We must stop playing hooky from our most basic of obligations to them, namely loving them unconditionally, nurturing them as they grow up, and equipping them for success in life. Urban Leaguers are fond of saying that *Our Children = Our Destiny.* That compelling slogan won't come alive unless we, the parents and caregivers who raise them, make it real by taking charge of ensuring that our children achieve.

# CHAPTER TWO

## *Spreading the Gospel of Achievement*

"Some black kids will shoot you down if you're smart in school and accuse you of having 'airs' and thinking you're better than anyone else. I love school but I don't want people to say stupid things about me or leave me out. It's hard to know what to do."

That chilling comment by Cheryl, a fifth-grader from Detroit, goes right to the heart of one of the biggest obstacles facing youngsters who want to do well in school. They can handle the schoolwork itself. But they struggle to fend off—and sometimes fall prey to—the intense razzing and sometimes even intimidation by schoolmates and friends who say they shouldn't be about achievement.

"Peer pressure is incredible," says Karla Ballard, a 30-year-old in Wilmington, Delaware, who helped found the National Urban League Young Professionals. Its purpose is to present positive role models to young people in the African-American community. "I was brought up in a single-parent household by my mother, who was a social worker and nurse. I attended public schools in Philadelphia until the fifth grade, then went to a private school. I lived in the inner city and the students at the prep school lived in the suburbs with big houses and cars. . . . Some of the neighborhood kids accused me of acting white because of the way I talked and how I looked."

Boys probably catch it worse than girls. "Being smart is looked down on," says Oscar, a soft-spoken 15-year-old achiever from New York. "My friends can't understand when I want to study instead of hanging out with them. They accuse me of selling out, acting 'white,' and talking 'proper.' Even though their words hurt, my dream is to go to college and I won't let anything stand in my way."

Even girls have noticed that boys come under more intense pressure. "Boys don't want to be 'nerds,' which smart boys are considered," according to Tiffany, a high school student in Atlanta. "It's easier for me and my friends, although we have the issue of appearing as snobs or kids telling us that we think we're better than anyone else because we get good grades and make our schoolwork our focus."

Parents who keep close tabs on their kids spot the problem as well. "My daughter always gets, 'You talk so proper. You sound like a teacher,'" says Helen, a teacher herself from Boston. "Then I get, 'Your daughter talks proper, just like you.' I offer no apologies for that. Instead, I say, 'Thank you.'"

*Education Week* reporter Debra Viadero quotes one shrewd parent who offers an intriguing theory as to why nonachievers try to drag other youngsters down with them. "It sounds like a defense mechanism to me," said Roslyn Mack, the mother of two African-American students attending integrated schools in the Cleveland suburb of Shaker Heights. "It gets reduced to: because I'm not doing well, I'm going to make you feel badly because you *are* doing well."

Some busy or oblivious parents may actually be unaware of the pressure on their youngsters to take their studies lightly. Things happen on playgrounds and among classmates that children keep to themselves. But the fact they don't complain doesn't make the pressure any less real. If they feel the pressure, but don't discuss it, that may actually make matters worse because it stays bottled inside them.

Even parents who are tuned in to their children struggle to motivate them to excel in school. "My son doesn't want to be the brightest kid in his class," complains a frustrated mother from St. Louis. "He wants to fit in. I keep on stressing that everyone is different, that it's better to be a leader than a follower. But that doesn't seem to hold much weight with a seven-year-old."

Sad to say, this peer pressure isn't an isolated problem. It seems to be especially intense in the black community. A researcher at Harvard, Ronald F. Ferguson, found in a 1999 study that black and white students had distinctly different ideas about what it takes to be popular. For instance, being tough was rated high among black adolescents while white youngsters rated that characteristic low. Yet their attitudes reversed toward academics. White students ranked being self-confident and outgoing in academic matters highly, while black students gave that a low rating.

In a study that stirred up lots of controversy in the mid-1980s, two scholars named John Ogbu and Signithia Fordham described how some low-achieving black high school students disparaged academic success as "acting white." The pressure knows no boundaries. It's present in racially mixed and predominantly minority schools, inner-city, and suburban schools alike.

Reporter Debra Viadero writes that some students equate academic success with "acting white," particularly if successful black students use standard English or socialize with white classmates in the hallways or outside of school. Some minority students say they steer away from tougher classes because, typical of adolescents, they want to be with their friends.

Children who succumb to this anti-achievement pressure do poorly in school. That in turn undermines their long-term chances for success in life. Why? The reason is simple. They fall so far behind the eight ball academically that they aren't adequately prepared for college, trade schools, or jobs, assuming they ever graduate from high school.

Here, too, things are worse for African-American males. They lag way behind white males when it comes to completing college and earning undergraduate science degrees, advanced degrees, and Ph.D.s. African-American women are roaring ahead as well. Even though more black men attend college than ever, with each passing year proportionately more women than men are enrolling, graduating, and going on to earn graduate and professional degrees. In fact, by the time they reach graduate school, black women outnumber black men more than two to one.

Say what black boys may about achievement not being cool, these widening disparities are calamitous for the African-American community. Educated black women search futilely for mates they can marry. Undereducated men who cannot qualify for good jobs barely stay afloat financially, and should they ever marry, they then struggle to shoulder their fair share of the family's financial burdens.

Peer pressure is a strong force in a child's life. Quite naturally, kids want to fit in with their friends. They crave being accepted by their peers as popular and cool, or whatever word for being "with it" is in at the time.

No adult I know wants a child they're raising to be unpopular, a loner, or isolated from friends. Still, this negative peer pressure can be so destructive that parents and caregivers must try as best they can to nip it in the bud the moment they spot signs that it's poisoning their child's attitude toward school. Instilling an eternal love of learning and an appreciation for education is one of the most valuable and durable gifts we can bestow on the loved ones we bring into this world.

## STRONG FAMILY SUPPORT + STRENGTH OF CHARACTER = SUCCESS

The illustrious educator and late president of Morehouse College, Dr. Benjamin Mays, once said: "It's not a disgrace not to reach for the stars, but it is a disgrace to have no stars to reach for."

If ever there's an area where parents and caregivers are indispensable, it's encouraging their children to dream, helping them chart a course to fulfill their dreams, and fending off temptations and forces that could derail them. Through abiding love and encouragement, parents enable youngsters to build the self-confidence and strength of character they'll need to navigate over, under, and around all the obstacles that could defeat them.

The first defense against negative peer pressure is for parents to believe in their children's potential from day one and set lofty goals for them early on. Don't aim so high at the outset that the odds are stacked sky high against them. If they're destined to become president, break barriers or climb mountaintops that will materialize later on as their ability, ambitions, and opportunities come together to shape their careers. Infancy is much too early for parents to declare that this daughter is going to be a lawyer or that son will become a doctor. Young people must make those decisions that profoundly shape their lives.

As a parent, I had a very basic goal for my daughters. I wanted each of them to grow up to become well-adjusted, well-educated, and well-informed citizens of the United States and the world who would be equipped to provide a comfortable life for themselves and their families. That kind of simple yet compelling goal gets child rearing off on the right track. It shows why education is critically important. That's because without a solid education, this goal simply cannot be met.

As youngsters mature and develop minds of their own, I believe that we should set subsequent goals with them, not for them. Better yet, we should help them to set their own goals that are suited to their unique personalities, aspirations, and sense of self.

Notice I stressed setting goals "with" them instead of "for" them. I say this because if parents aren't careful, they can be overbearing about setting goals for another human being, no matter how young. Placing unbearable pressure on children can dampen their creativity, dull their spontaneity, and, carried to extremes, even rob them of their childhood. That serves no purpose and could spark resentment toward school.

When I speak of spreading the gospel of achievement, I don't use the word "gospel" lightly. As Velma Cobb, director of the National

Urban League's Campaign for African-American Achievement, observes: "There is almost a spiritual element for the children in our academic achievement efforts. Our philosophy is rooted in the core belief that children are ready and willing to learn. We emphasize pride in achievement, we give them recognition, and they have a connection and feeling that they are part of something bigger. Peers are important on all levels. By getting educated, you set yourself apart. 'Are you saying you're better than me?' is what children hear from their friends. We understand that kids don't want to be different, but if their friends are smart and achievers, that's another matter entirely."

Many youngsters have the inner strength to distance themselves from friends who don't share their commitment to academic success. The adults who've raised them deserve much of the credit. That proven formula—*strong family support + strength of character = success*—explains why Jared, a seventh-grader from Philadelphia, does so well in school. He's been enrolled in honor programs and advanced classes ever since he can remember. "If you're intelligent, you can get hit on and beaten up," Jared says. "But my grandmother says you can't let others pull you down. She says that education is the most important thing in the world." Or as another Philadelphia teenager whose compass is set squarely on achievement put it: "You have to do what's best for yourself. Don't worry about what others think of you. Just continue to be diligent and dedicated."

Karla Ballard reminds us that mentors who aren't family members also can play a critical role in helping youngsters fend off negative influences from peers who aren't about education. "African-American children . . . connect like magnets very fast to an interested adult," she observes. "Being a concerned parent, caregiver, or in my case a mentor to many young people, helps build a child's self-esteem, which he or she can then use as a shield of armor against peer pressure. If we raise the level of expectation for our children, it shows them how much we value them."

Research shows that youngsters whose real friends do well in school generally do well themselves. That's because this network of academically successful friends provides a protective cover, so to speak, for youngsters who want to excel as well. A young Meyerhoff Scholar named George described how important peer support can be: "I went to a math and science magnet high school, and there were only a handful of African Americans in my class. We became very tight and motivated each other. We felt we had to represent our race, and do very well just to be equal."

Parents usually know who their children's closest friends are because they play together after school at each other's homes. But that larger network of schoolmates they're exposed to and take signals from—and may even be intimidated by—can be a total mystery. Parents who want their children to be achievers seldom encounter those shadowy peers who don't care about school, who accuse their black classmates of acting "white," taunt them mercilessly, and perhaps even threaten them if they do well academically. This intimidation leads youngsters to hold back in class, hide their ability, earn lowly grades so they never show up on the honor roll, perform poorly on exams, even shy away from accepting academic awards at school assemblies.

Whom your child befriends is your business. Seek out other families that share your values and instill them in their children as well. When I was a kid, groups like the Brownies, Boy Scouts, and Sunday school class seemed pretty corny. Little did I realize how important they were to my parents and to me. Why? Because they drew youngsters into a peer group that embraced positive values.

So make a point of enrolling your child in programs where they meet and become buddies with other youngsters who enjoy learning and care about doing well in school. Contact the local Boy Scouts and Girl Scouts, Boys and Girls Clubs, Urban Leagues, YMCA and YWCA, and community centers to see if they offer a youth program that your child can join. Enroll them in youth programs at your church. Check with the Eastern Star and the Masons to see if they operate youth auxiliaries. By joining groups like these, your child will develop a set of friends who are dedicated to academic success.

# SETTING THE TONE FOR ACHIEVEMENT

A couple of weeks after our youngest daughter turned thirty, my wife and I were sitting around the breakfast table with her, reminiscing about her childhood. At some point the conversation turned to the fact that I was writing this book. My daughter asked whether I intended to deal with the whole issue of how adults, like parents and teachers, talk to children. I replied that I hadn't planned to, in part because that topic struck me as a bit outside my focus on academic achievement.

My daughter pressed her question by pointing out that the tone that adults set in conversing with kids can affect how they feel about themselves and about school, both of which could have a direct bearing on how well they do academically. She went on to recount a personal experience that really drove home her point.

All through school, she reminded us, she was reticent about speaking up in class. She worked hard to overcome her hesitancy, but oral participation in class never came easily. Anyway, when she was just five years old, her teacher exclaimed to her in a raised voice and exasperated tone, "Why don't you speak up!" The harshness of the comment startled my daughter. Far from encouraging her to be more vocal, the teacher's criticism had exactly the opposite effect, making this young and impressionable child even quieter in class. Instead of supporting and encouraging my daughter when she could have used it, the teacher had shaken her confidence, which is the very last thing a teacher who cares about kids should do.

Educators aren't the only culprits. Parents and relatives can be just as unsupportive and verbally abusive, even physically abusive in all-too-many instances. I've heard some parents call their children stupid to their face, in a voice loud enough for others to hear. For kids, that kind of devastating put-down by adults who are important figures in their lives can cause them to strike back, act out, or crawl into a shell. It certainly doesn't instill the kind of enthusiasm for school that produces high achievers.

As Dr. James P. Comer wrote in his insightful book, *Waiting for a Miracle,* youngsters need to be developed and nurtured, not denigrated and dismissed by the important adults in their lives. This should begin the day they're born. According to Dr. Comer, "As parents of newborns hold and talk to them, a warm feeling begins to develop between the parent and the child. The parents take care of the child's food, clothing, safety, and comfort needs. The physical and language connection, emotional warmth, and comfort reduce the trauma of birth. Such care begins to produce what will eventually become a deep-seated inner sense of security and well-being in the child. 'I am' begins here.

"They [children] are born with only biological and behavioral potentials (including a capacity for relationship) and aggressive and survival energies. The aggressive or survival energy can be destructive unless it is channeled and brought under the child's personal control. The relationship capacity makes it possible for caretakers to protect children from themselves and others—to limit their destructive potentials."

If they don't know it beforehand, Dr. Comer cautions us, parents need to realize that "[s]ocializing children is a long, tough journey. But somebody has to do it. For this reason, it is important for children to be born into a family in which they are wanted. And parents must have the resources and skills to help their children develop.

"But parents under economic, social, and psychological stress—parents with less access to opportunities—more often have difficulties with children. Despite good intentions and sometimes remarkable efforts, their care of children often ranges from marginal to abusive. 'I am' starts here, too. Sustained bad care eventually leads to a deep-seated inner sense of insecurity and inadequacy, emotional pain, and a troublesome sense of self."

The remarkable Maggie Comer recalled seeing firsthand what her son was writing about. "Many people the only time they talk to them is when they holler at them. 'Get away from me, boy, I don't have time, I'm washing' or 'I'm ironing,' or they don't have a reason—just 'Get away, I just don't want to be bothered; don't have time.' 'Go sit down, shut up.' Now shut up, that's a famous one."

Not surprisingly, verbal and physical abuse by adults takes a severe toll on youthful victims that becomes more debilitating over time. It gradually drains children of their self-confidence and their dreams. Dr. Comer continues: "I observed a nine-year-old child at an airport who had accompanied his mother and siblings to welcome a relative home. In the bright spirit of inquiry, maybe teasing because he knew better, he wondered aloud what would happen if he told the guards at the metal detector that he had a gun. His mother angrily said, 'Shut up or I'll smack you in the mouth.' The look of curiosity and fun fell, and he moved to the back of the group, crushed. There was no patient lesson about appropriate time and place or harmful consequences. The child just got put down and controlled.

"In the office of my optometrist in a low-income area, a very large woman tried to get her bright-eyed, playful, provocative son to sit in his chair. He was humming, exploring, enjoying himself. He maneuvered just outside the range of her chair. But when he moved too close, in a flash she snatched him and slapped him to the ground with one powerful blow. . . . The doctor told me that the woman had been his patient since childhood. He told me of the abuse and anger she had endured as a child, and was inflicting in turn on her child. The mother clearly did not have high expectations for her child. But to my eyes this was a smart little rascal. For reasons that have nothing to do with intelligence, punitive behavior is the more frequent approach of less-educated people."

The emotional damage caused by abuse can undermine children's interest in school and their desire to do well. As Dr. Comer notes: "Relying on punishment and control rather than discussion and support for responsible behavior tends to limit the exploration of ideas and independent thinking. Young people who can't examine ideas may be misled by opportunists and hatemongers. The capacity for independent thinking can best be developed in a child-rearing process that promotes inner control. It requires a gradual allowance of greater freedom and participation in decision making for children as they demonstrate their ability to make good decisions and manage increased freedom responsibly."

Just as parents who were verbally or physically abused when they were young have been known to dish it out to their own children, so the children who are victimized often become abusive toward others around them, youngsters and adults alike. This creates a vicious cycle of aggressive behavior that keeps youngsters from achieving and often earns them an undeserved one-way ticket to special education.

As Dr. Comer reminds us, "Many children have learned to fight because they have not been taught to negotiate for what they want. Some have been told that they will get a beating at home if they don't fight when they are challenged—a catch-22 that only gets them into trouble at school. Teachers too often punish them and hold low expectations for them rather than help them grow along developmental pathways where most mainstream parents have led their children before school."

Abused children behave in ways that alienate them from teachers and other students. Academic achievement recedes as a priority or a reality for them. Gradually they drop out of school, mentally if not physically. According to Dr. Comer: "Unprepared but otherwise good children respond to punishment by fighting back, particularly when the relationship between the teacher and child is not positive. They fight for power and control through teasing and provocation, just as mainstream children do. The struggle is for the same prize—autonomy and identity. The usual response at school is to clamp down on the children. . . . In such struggles children sometimes gain mastery of skills that are self-defeating in the long run, such as manipulation, dishonesty, and ignoring the rights of others.

"Some children respond in an opposite way: self-doubt grows and they give up and withdraw. Afraid to take risks, they shun the mental exploration they need for academic achievement. These students are often neglected while teachers attend to more vociferous kids. If they are as timid socially as academically, they are also neglected by their peers, increasing their sense of isolation.

"Most will not continue to develop so as to achieve their social and academic potential. Most go on a downhill course and repeat the marginal experience of their parents, despite the fact that almost all parents want their children to succeed in school and in life," concludes Dr. Comer.

That is the tragedy in all this. It reminds me of that famous saying: "With friends like these, who needs enemies." Abusive parents who instinctively want their children to succeed and insensitive educators whose job is to help them achieve unwittingly team up to destroy children's self-confidence and dash their dreams. In the hearts and minds of children, tone matters if we expect achievement to be valued as well.

## THE PERILS OF STEREOTYPES AND CELEBRITY CULTURE

Negative stereotypes in the minds of adults can be just as destructive as negative pressure from the mouths of peers. "Many adults and teachers looked at me and judged me based on my skin color," says Elijah, a 20-year-old father of two from New Haven. "Maybe they didn't say it outright but I got the message that I was expected to be disinterested in school work and only interested in gangs, drugs, and hanging out. I started believing it myself and I lost interest in school and I stopped trying to do well."

When I visit the neighborhoods served by Urban League affiliates in cities around the country, I see block upon block of hard-working parents who want the best for their children. Yet there's a harmful and erroneous image out there that all black kids care about is listening to rap music, playing hoops, wearing "gangsta" fashions, and hanging out with idle friends who are up to no good.

Karla Ballard is convinced that teachers have lower expectations for black students than for their white classmates and therefore demand less from them. "It becomes a self-fulfilling prophecy," she says. "It's very different growing up as an African American than in the white culture. I remember in third grade having to take reading tests and being very frightened. I felt as if I were being judged about my intelligence purely on tests, and felt incredible pressure to prove myself."

According to the authors of *Beating the Odds,* educators develop impressions of black children's ability and potential early on based on their performance in elementary school and how they score on standardized exams. If youngsters detect negative attitudes and low expectations from their teachers, as a defense mechanism they may write themselves off academically before they are written off by the school system. They then look to street culture for the alternative terms of success, and to gangs and ne'er-do-wells for acceptance and approval.

"It's interesting to see how teachers react to us when we're wearing our ties," says a sixth-grader who participates in an after-school program, known as the Club, for black boys in middle school. The Club was founded and is financed by the Westchester Clubmen, a suburban men's group outside of New York City that I've belonged to for years. "They think of us differently when we're dressed up," this young member of the Club added. "I don't think there's anything really different between white kids and us, but the teachers sometimes don't act that way."

Rap music is another source of anti-achievement messages that young people hear. Mind you, I'm not condemning all rap musicians. Many rappers couple biting social commentary with positive lyrics about how to improve things. Still, there's no question that some rappers see only the dark side of life and dismiss trying to succeed on society's terms. That message is ruinous and leads nowhere.

How to handle this is a tricky issue for adults who care, as they should, about the messages their youngsters hear and absorb. If parents aren't careful, this generation gap can make things worse. "Keep it real," cautions Alicia, a design student from the South Bronx. "It doesn't do anything just to be against the music your kids like. It's better to understand it."

Alicia explains that when she was growing up, her role model was Martin Luther King. "Now, kids have different role models," she says. "Some are anti-achievement. But I also think that if you use the media they're interested in, for example, gangsta rap, to analyze the lyrics with them, you can understand their world better. My mother used my brother's love for rap music to communicate with him. She had him write out the lyrics for her to understand and then they talked about them together."

Our children grow up in a culture that is obsessed with celebrity. They are seduced into believing that there are shortcuts to success and that earning less than $1 million a year is the minimum wage. I exaggerate, of course. But I am reminded of a story told me by a friend who runs a community foundation. He joined with several professional friends to start a mentoring program for black teenage boys from an inner-city neighborhood.

After a few sessions, the youngsters asked how much money the mentors make. The men, who counted lawyers, corporate executives, and doctors among them, went around the room. If I recall correctly, their incomes ranged from $100,000 to $250,000 or so. The response by the teenagers floored them. "How do you get over," the youngsters asked, "on $150,000 a year?" The youngsters weren't the least bit impressed by these hefty salaries given all they'd heard about the multimillion-dollar contracts of athletes and entertainers.

Some immensely talented—and lucky and driven—people soar into the stratosphere in terms of celebrity status and wealth. Education is useful, but hardly instrumental to their success. But adults who live in the real world understand that these superstars are the rare exception, and hardly the rule. While it's fine for our children to have heroes, we must bring their expectations down to earth without crushing their spirit. They need everyday role models to reach for. In this day and age, education will be key to the success of almost any role model they're likely to pick.

"You don't have a future if you don't have a degree," says Harold, an eighth-grader from Detroit. "If you blow your knee playing sports, you'll still have an education. Some of my friends like school, but some think they'll make it in the pros. Athletics sometimes seem more important than an education and it can become confusing."

It's okay for our children to fantasize of being the next Michael Jordan or Tiger Woods or Destiny's Child. In my early teens, there was no doubt in my mind whatsoever that I'd become a major league baseball player. Still, my very wise parents made sure I knew there were other routes to success, just in case I couldn't hit a curveball, which it turned out I couldn't. There are so many fascinating people and fields of work. Use libraries, field trips, the Internet, and documentaries on TV to expose your child to the vast career possibilities that are wide open to them if they're well educated and willing to work hard to achieve their goals.

## CELEBRATING ACHIEVEMENT

Parents shouldn't have to combat this negative peer pressure by themselves. Community groups can get into the act of spreading the gospel of achievement and thereby envelope children in a culture that values academic success. That's exactly what the National Urban League set out to do when we launched the Campaign for African-American Achievement in 1996.

We enlisted organizations in the Campaign that have been fixtures in the black community for generations and that will be there generations from now. I speak of groups like the Congress of National Black Churches and its eight major religious denominations; sororities and fraternities; and civic, social, and professional organizations. You'll notice that the other distinctive feature of our Achievement Campaign partners is that they have vast memberships of mothers and fathers and other relatives who are raising children.

Right from the outset, we trained our sights smack on the problem of negative peer pressure. Knowing how vital education is in this day and age, we decided that the black community couldn't—and wouldn't—tolerate that anti-achievement peer culture any longer. We had to create a vibrant new atmosphere in our community that values and celebrates academic achievement. No longer, we vowed, would children who want to achieve be ignored by adults or intimidated by schoolmates.

We chose several ways to go about creating this new mind-set in the community and among our children. For starters, we were struck by the fact that cities often mounted parades to celebrate their sports champions, but never their scholastic champs. So on the third Saturday of September across the country, Urban League affiliates and their local Achievement Campaign partners staged events like block parties, street festivals, and even a parade or two right through downtown to recognize young people who are "doing the right thing." By that we mean performing well in school and serving their communities in some way.

The point of these high-profile events is to mobilize adults to send positive signals to youngsters about the kind of behavior we value and, frankly, to encourage the news media to cover these kinds of kids for a change. Each year since we started in 1996, these events have drawn upwards of 50,000 to 60,000 youngsters around the country. They are magnets for media coverage. Viewers of all ages get to see positive stories about young people on the evening news. That's a welcome change from the endless diet of stories about young drug addicts and stickup artists.

The enthusiastic response of young people to these celebrations warms the heart. It shows how receptive youngsters are to the message that achievement matters when adults say it to them loudly enough, often enough, and lovingly enough.

I'll never forget a youngster who nearly accosted me immediately following a "Doing the Right Thing" rally at Martin Luther King High School in New York City. He was upset that he wasn't up on stage with the other honorees even though, he said, he'd done everything we were looking for. "Keep at it," I urged him, "we'll catch you next year." In my experience, many more youngsters would resist all the razzing by friends and strive to achieve if only we'd support them, encourage them, and recognize them this way.

The second approach we've used successfully in the Campaign to spread the gospel of achievement is our National Achievers Society. It's sort of a community-based honor society for students who've earned B averages or better in school. As much as I'd like to take credit for this fabulous idea, I cannot because it didn't originate with me or even with the Achievement Campaign, for that matter.

It started out in Florida in the mid-1980s, the brainchild of Dr. Israel Tribble. He's the former president of the Florida Education Fund, an outfit that provides scholarships to minority college students to pursue doctorate degrees in math and science.

Ike, as friends like me affectionately call him, is as passionate and determined as any person I've ever known about promoting academic excellence in minority children. Anyway, he reached out to several Urban League affiliates in Florida with the inspired idea that they create this community-based honor society and join forces with the religious community to conduct annual induction ceremonies in churches. Originally the initiative was called the McKnight Achievers Society, named after a local benefactor.

Soon after I took the job as president of the National Urban League, I visited the dynamic Urban League of Broward County, Florida. In an experience I'll never forget, I was inducted as an honorary member of Broward's chapter of the McKnight Achievers Society. I stored that experience in my memory bank because instinct told me that this was a powerful concept that deserved to spread across the country.

When we launched the Achievement Campaign, we got permission from Dr. Tribble and the Florida affiliates to take their idea national. We ended up naming it the National Achievers Society. As of 2001, there were two-dozen chapters around the country. Since 1997 when we staged the first induction in Washington, D.C., with Colin Powell as the keynote speaker, we've admitted more than 10,000 achievers to the ranks of the National Achievers Society. We've also recognized thousands of youthful "believers" who yearn to become "achievers" but haven't quite earned the grades to qualify.

To win induction into the National Achievers Society, students must:

- Be in the third to twelfth grade.
- Earn a B average or better.
- Make all A's or B's, with no C's unless they are in advanced honors courses.
- Be sponsored by an adult who will serve as a mentor or role model in the achiever's life.

The induction ceremony itself is something to behold. In June of 2001, I flew out to San Diego for their induction ceremony. Bayview Baptist Church overflowed with 800 parents and relatives; so many, in fact, that some people had to sit in the pews reserved for the church choir.

That glorious Saturday afternoon in Southern California, the San Diego Urban League and its Campaign partners inducted 350 brilliant young achievers in a moving ceremony. Looking out over the audience, I rejoiced at the fact that half of the inductees were boys.

The young men and women who were beaming with pride there before me obviously weren't buying that nonsense that being bright is acting white. The local newspapers and television stations loved the story. So hundreds and, by now, thousands of parents, caregivers, and kids have definitely begun reciting the gospel of achievement out in San Diego.

A year earlier I attended the induction ceremony at Metropolitan Missionary Baptist Church in Kansas City, Missouri. Picture this. On the Saturday before Mother's Day, the Kansas City Urban League, under the inspired leadership of its late CEO, the Rev. William Clark, joined with its Achievement Campaign partners in inducting 150 high school achievers. They also recognized another 200 "believers" from elementary and middle school who were "wannabe" achievers.

Packed into the pews of the church that afternoon were 1,300 parents, grandparents, siblings, and teachers, cheering those achievers on. Seventeen hundred people in all, there for the sole purpose of celebrating stellar academic achievement by black children. And note this: Nearly 40 percent of the youngsters inducted that day were boys.

The ceremony itself was inspiring. The inductees marched up to the front of the church, where they were introduced individually and their accomplishments were read off to the rapt audience. Then each inductee was presented with a customized National Achievers Society jacket that conferred privileged status on the members. Once they had all been recognized and robed, the inductees recited the National Achievers Society pledge that committed them to continue down the path of high achievement.

> *I am excellent. I am excellent. I am excellent.*
> *My mind is a pearl. I can do anything.*
> *Anything that my mind can conceive, I can achieve.*
> *Anything that my mind can conceive and my heart can*
> *believe, I can achieve.*
> *I am excellent. I am excellent. I am a National Achiever.*

Contact your local Urban League to find out if there's a chapter of the National Achievers Society in your town. If so, you might ask for information about it and take your children to an induction ceremony so they can see how the achievers are celebrated and cheered on. That could inspire them to excel in school so that someday they will be eligible for induction.

If there isn't an achievers society nearby, then appeal to churches and civic groups to create something like it locally that mobilizes parents and community people to recognize academic achievers in this way. Winning induction into the Honor Society at school is a huge honor. But experience with the National Achievers Society has shown me that recognition by the community—by the churches and groups that families members and friends actually belong to—adds special meaning and motivation to young people who are trying to muster the courage to go for it academically.

What we've done with the National Achievers Society, in effect, is to create a "National Achievement Gang" that youngsters are clamoring to join. This gang has its own rituals and regalia, its own credo and colors. It's what's on their report cards, not how much is in their wallets, that matters. The exclusive jacket they receive can't be bought at a sporting goods store. Excellent grades are the only currency that matters. We challenge the members to spread the gospel of achievement to their sisters, brothers, cousins, and friends.

These impressive young people are the toast of the town in their communities. They know it and they know the reason why—because they've truly taken the gospel of achievement to heart.

There are other ways as well to promote achievement. For instance, in recent years the National Urban League has partnered with State Farm Life Insurance Company to spread the message that "Achievement Matters." Together State Farm and the Urban League have run ads in African-American newspapers, mounted this message on billboards, and placed posters on city buses. Local State Farm offices and our affiliates sponsor achievement rallies in schools that are attended by hundreds of students.

In Columbia, South Carolina, the local Urban League and the insurance company teamed up to stage an SAT awareness rally. The idea was to help black high school students understand why this college entrance exam was so important in their lives and how they could prepare themselves to do well on it. The Urban League originally expected a couple hundred students to turn out. Lo and behold, nearly seven hundred actually showed up. And get this. Coverage of the rally was the lead story on the six o'clock and eleven o'clock television newscasts that night. Plus public television carried the entire event. So viewers of all ages and races were treated that night to the sight of nearly one thousand black students who were as serious as a heartbeat about advancing themselves via education.

Concerted efforts like these help shape impressionable young minds and persuade students that achievement is cool. For instance, State Farm and the Urban League commissioned a survey of students who'd been exposed to the ads, billboards, and assemblies that I mentioned earlier. While I don't want to make too much of the results, we were delighted by what we found. The survey suggests that we actually are turning youngsters on to learning—and to achieving in school. The young people told us:

- Their grades and attendance in school improved as a result of participating in the achievement campaign.
- They're more inclined to be on time to class.
- They're more likely now to use a computer, bring their textbooks home, do their daily homework, and do so with fewer distractions from television or CDs.
- They're more interested in going on to college or other forms of education after high school, and thus more likely to register to take college entrance exams.

My roughly forty years of firsthand experience as a parent, a professional youth worker, a volunteer mentor, an Urban Leaguer, and a founder of the Campaign for African-American Achievement convinces me beyond a shadow of a doubt that we can turn our children on to academic achievement. Equally important, it's imperative that we do so. If we allow our young people to grow up believing that academic achievement is above them, beneath them, or beside the point, then we've failed them as parents and as a society. It's the mission in life of anyone who has created life to equip children for success through education.

## PROMOTE PRIDE IN OUR ACCOMPLISHMENTS

When I was growing up in the late 1940s and early 1950s, the public schools in Washington, D.C., were segregated. So I was required to attend an all-black elementary school. The walls of the central corridor at Blanche K. Bruce School where I went were decorated with pictures and brief stories about celebrated heroes in the history of the African-American people. At an early age, I became very proud of the accomplishments of my people.

Along with learning what they had contributed to our people

and to society at large, I also came to realize from reading about them how important education was to what they had achieved. Of course, that wasn't true of some of the athletes, like heavyweight boxing champions Jack Johnson and Joe Louis, who were our heroes. But even some of the pioneers in sport—such as Jackie Robinson, the first black man to play major league baseball, and Jesse Owens, the gold medal winner at the 1936 Olympics in Hitler's Germany—were college educated. Higher education definitely helped pave the way for their success.

Most of the stories on the wall at my school, however, weren't about sports stars. B. K. Bruce, the black man elected to the U.S. Senate after the Civil War ended, was up there, of course. So was Ralph Bunche, who won the Nobel Prize for Peace. Along with Dr. George Washington Carver, the scientist and inventor, and Frederick Douglass, the fiery orator and freedom fighter. There were Benjamin Bannecker, who laid out the street grid system in the nation's capital, and Harriett Tubman, a major force behind the Underground Railroad that shepherded escaped slaves to freedom up north.

Missing from the walls, though, were the noted French novelist Alexandre Dumas and celebrated Russian poet Aleksandr Pushkin. Why? Because it wasn't known, or at least it wasn't acknowledged, back then that they had some African ancestors. With all the civil rights luminaries, visionary entrepreneurs, legendary educators, political leaders, and corporate pioneers who've made notable contributions over the last half century since I was in elementary school, that gallery of heroes today would now have to wind its way throughout the entire school. And to bring the concept of accomplishment even closer to home, I think schools should include stories about local heroes who've contributed to the community or done noble deeds, such as running a mentoring program. Youngsters need to know that you don't have to be a headliner in order to be a hero.

Pride in the accomplishments of one's people, especially those accomplishments where education is key, can be a powerful tool for motivating young people to achieve in school. That's why educators, parents, and community leaders should insist that school curriculum take full and fair account of the immense contributions by people of color to shaping American society and world culture. This kind of content should also be built into the curricula of Sunday schools, after-school programs, and even activities that parents do with their children.

Mind you, I don't endorse multiculturalism because of some hazy belief that schools must boost students' self-esteem. No. I'm convinced it's critically important for schools to give an accurate accounting of all the forces that have shaped the nation's history and culture. That will open youngsters' eyes to what people just like them can accomplish and contribute, sometimes even against steep odds, provided they obtain an education.

Janie Victoria Ward, author of *The Skin We're In: Teaching Our Children to Be Emotionally Strong, Socially Smart, and Spiritually Connected,* really drives home this point when she says: "By teaching the history of black folks' struggle for education, often by sharing our personal stories of what family members have had to endure to gain admission to our nation's schools and colleges, parents teach their children that they are connected to a long line of people who have refused to allow others to shape their destiny. We can also teach our children that they have a personal and collective responsibility to honor connections and to do their best."

Appreciating African-American history can provide black children with a cultural grounding, a kind of building block of learning, according to educator Moleifi Kete Asante. Children who lack this cultural foundation, he believes, become alienated, which can sour them on the importance of education for the rest of their lives.

"We can see the results of this deprivation in the listlessness with which too many of our children approach their school work, and the speed with which they turn away from it," Mr. Asante writes. "We can see it in the verbal disrespect and rough behavior they exhibit toward teachers and each other. We can see it in the low opinion they have of themselves, and in the lack of vision they have about their future."

In raising their children, parents and caregivers need to emphasize over and over that education is key to ensuring their future and fulfilling their dreams. Since racial discrimination lingers to this day in education and the workplace, that's all the more reason why minority children must take education seriously. It's the great equalizer in our society.

As Janie Victoria puts it in her book, "[P]arents . . . need to be brutally honest with their teenagers about the grave consequences of an inadequate education for black people: poverty, social and political disenfranchisement . . . and further marginalization."

## WHAT ELSE YOU CAN DO

Responsibility for spreading the gospel of achievement begins right at home. Encourage family members to work as a team and take responsibility for creating a learning environment within the home. Introduce your children to the joys of learning and discovery from the time they are toddlers. Play games and do projects together that help them see how enjoyable educationally oriented activities can be. As they enter preschool and approach kindergarten, start talking up school as an important yet enjoyable place to go. Help them see from the day they enroll why doing well is a good thing and how much pride you take in their performance.

As your children move on through elementary school, urge them to pay no attention to classmates who say academics aren't important. Get family members on the same page so that every adult and older sibling whom your child looks to for love and support, guidance and advice is preaching the gospel of achievement.

Talk to your children about your own experiences in school, even if they weren't always happy and even if you didn't do well. Having grown up and seen how the world works, you are wiser now. Now you can see more clearly than when you were growing up why education is key to success. As you look at how job requirements have changed, you've seen up close how education has become more and more important with each passing year.

Twelve-year-old Kujo Gabrielle of New York City has it right when he says: "It's important for parents to let us know what they've been through, so we can identify. When a kid is smart, you're like a nerd and that can be scary. Focus and forget everyone is there," he advises. "If not, you'll be looking at them looking at you. There will be friends who will stay with you. But you don't want to brag either. You have to have a balance."

The authors of *Beating the Odds: Raising Academically Successful African American Males* stress how important it is to speak to your children in a way that doesn't leave them feeling bitter or like helpless victims. There should be family discussions that focus on how to survive and how to thrive within society. "We need to empower our children to see the connection between hard work and success," Dr. Hrabrowski and his coauthors write. "The discussion can include whomever the adults consider to be 'family' and central to the children's achievements."

To sum up, parents and caregivers should:

• **Have high expectations for your children and refuse to accept anything less.**

Don't fall for the nonsense that rigorous academic courses aren't for your child. Studies show that far fewer black and Latino children take tough courses than white children. Youngsters know when they're being deprived. "A lot of times, I think blacks are discouraged from being in honors or advanced placement classes because they see no one else of their race in those classes," says Imani Farley, an African-American tenth-grader at Shaker Heights High School in Ohio. "And sometimes counselors don't encourage you to challenge yourself." Don't let the schools get away with it. Stand up for your child's right to the best education available.

• **Communicate your love of learning to your children.**

Whether or not you were a good student yourself, as a parent you must be passionate about the importance of education and convey that passion early and often to your own children and to any other children in your lives. Our ancestors before us who were enslaved, illiterate, and discriminated against understood that education was key to advancing our people. If they could see its impor-

tance when confronted with so much adversity, surely we can see it
when faced with such opportunity.

• **Encourage your children to seek out friends who also are serious about school and are proud of their academic achievements.**

Student groups, extracurricular clubs, and after-school programs are the kinds of places where children can meet other students with the same interests. In addition, parents belong to churches,
sororities, fraternal orders, unions, and civic groups where they can
bring their children into contact with other families that share the
same values. As I've found with the Achievement Campaign, these
kinds of organizations can stage all sorts of activities—from group
trips to tutorial programs—that support learning and achievement.
These adult organizations are an important source of playmates
and support for your child.

"In school, I had good friends who did well but there were also
people who gave you a hard time if you were a good achiever. I
spoke well and did well and it wasn't considered cool," says
Candace Smith, 32, an attorney with a big law firm in Atlanta and
a member of the National Urban League's Board of Trustees. "I
would advise kids to find people like themselves, who have the
same values and feeling toward education. You have to find that support even after school, and need to seek out like-minded friends."

• **Get your child to take pride in being an achiever and see the
value of academic success.**

I believe all children want to do well in the eyes of those adults
who are important in their lives. I'm also convinced that when large
numbers of them fail, it's mostly because the key adults in their
lives—parents, relatives, schoolteachers, principals, and their larger
community—have failed to nurture them the way we should and
the way we know how. "Children must know that the commitment
and perseverance they put towards their academic, social, and civic
efforts will allow them to reap rewards that will benefit them for
years to come," says Bishop Cecil Bishop, head of the African
Methodist Episcopal Zion Church and chairman of the Congress of
National Black Churches, a founding partner in the Achievement

Campaign. "Young people must always aim high and keep their feet on solid ground."

This isn't to say that lousy schools aren't a problem. Obviously they are. This isn't to say that poverty isn't a problem. Clearly it is. It obviously makes day-to-day life really tough. It drains energy and hope from hard-pressed parents who struggle mightily to make ends meet. But lousy schools and low-income families aren't anything new. With perseverance and pride, vision and resolve, loving families have helped their children surmount these obstacles and achieve success. Communities that are committed to their children have provided them with the value system and support that enables them to move, in the inspiring words of historian Dr. Charles Wesley, "onward and upward toward the light."

"It's not where you start out, but where you end up," says Dr. Israel Tribble, godfather of the National Achievers Society. "And if the elevator to success is not working, take the stairs!"

# CHAPTER THREE

## Reading: The Bedrock of Academic Success

When I first told my eldest daughter that I was writing this book about what parents can do to help their children succeed in school, she chuckled. She was 36 at the time. She said she still remembered how, when she was really little, I would read to her every night before she fell asleep. Well over thirty years later, she could barely remember the stories themselves, but she'd never forgotten that my wife and I routinely read to her.

Why did we read to our children so much? At the time, we weren't aware of any research studies showing that reading to your children when they're very young helps set the stage for academic success once they're in school. My wife and I had a copy of Dr. Spock's famous book in our apartment when we were young parents. But to be perfectly honest about it, I don't recall ever reading his bible on child rearing. So you know I don't remember what it said about the importance of reading to your children.

What my wife and I did know instinctively is that we wanted to foster a love of reading and the joy of discovery that comes with it. We wanted our children to grow up seeing that we read a lot ourselves, that reading was a big deal in our household, and that we wanted them to cultivate a love of reading. We figured that if we read frequently to them, they would see how important we thought it was and that would stoke their interest. As a practical matter, this would help them begin to understand the symbols and sounds that form the basis for reading.

Now I'm the first to admit that since our parents were all college educated, we were just doing what comes naturally. Whatever the reason, we were simply doing way back then what all the researchers now tell us is exactly the right thing to do, regardless of whether we're educated or not.

As our children grew from toddlers to preschoolers, we bought them plenty of books. Their grandparents and aunts and uncles also gave them books galore. Not every family has the money to buy new books. But books can be passed around. Every family can get a library card and take out books for their children to read. The point is that it's essential to read to children early on, for them to see books and other reading material around the house, and for them to have books to read as their literacy skills begin to develop.

For heaven's sake, keep a close eye on how much television your children watch. Better yet, keep their eyes off of it as much as you can. Of course, there are some shows they probably should watch because of the educational value. The real problem these days is the huge quantity of television children watch. Studies show clearly that children who read well watch much less television, and spend more time interacting with their parents and siblings, reading, or engaging in other educationally beneficial activities.

When I was growing up in the late 1940s, televisions were just becoming popular and affordable enough for middle-class families to buy. We had this huge set with a tiny screen scarcely bigger than a saucer. The reception was so fuzzy that you'd get dizzy if you stayed glued to the tube too long. But no one in our house became a television addict. My mother paid it no mind whatsoever and hardly does to this day.

We used to eat dinner in midafternoon because my father, a physician, had to go back out for evening office hours. When he finally got home after a grueling day, Dad headed straight to the living room to read. He loved books about life close to nature by authors such as Henry David Thoreau and Lewis Bromfield. I was impressed by the fact that reading was his favorite way to relax.

I'm not as disciplined as Dad was. Plus I really enjoy watching pro sports such as baseball, basketball, and tennis on TV. Our daughters liked *Gumby.* We even encouraged our kids to watch *Mr. Rogers' Neighborhood* to help them chill out in late afternoon after a hard day of chasing around. So even in that precable, pre-MTV era, we could clock some serious time in front of the tube if we weren't careful. My wife set limits on how much our daughters could watch and made them pick the single hour's worth of programming they wanted to see after dinner on weeknights. Otherwise the TV was strictly off-limits during the week. They were expected to do schoolwork, play games, or read.

There was another device for limiting TV viewing that worked. When we lived on Ford Street in New Haven, our house was burgled a few times and we kept losing portable TVs to thieves. I eventually got fed up and bought a huge, secondhand floor model for about twenty-five bucks. I figured that if it was stolen, I'd just go around to the local hospitals to see who had checked in with a hernia that day and I'd have my crook. Anyway, these used TVs kept breaking down. We couldn't afford to fix them right away, and besides, it wasn't really worth the expense because they were already old. So we left them broken for months on end.

At first, it was a tough adjustment, at least for me. Everyone else adapted quite easily. Believe me, it's a revelation to see what happens to a television-free household. The conversation picks up, the kids get even more into reading, and most anything becomes an excuse for learning and discovery. It really was wonderful.

The rest of the family could have gone on like that forever. I was the one who got antsy as the pro basketball playoffs approached and I had to watch. So I'd invariably buy a cheap new portable television and tempt fate anew in exchange for the chance to watch hoops. The others slowly returned to the tube, but avoided getting completely hooked.

Unfortunately, television these days has become an electronic baby-sitter, especially after school while parents are working and even when they're right at home. It isn't elitist to say that the tube really does undermine reading and learning because so much time is consumed by watching it and so much information and so many images are handed to young viewers on a platter. Time spent passively in front of television is time not spent reading or broadening a child's horizons and hopes through the printed word.

No matter how busy or exhausted parents are at the end of the day, they shouldn't deposit their children in front of the television for hours at a time. You should limit the amount of television viewing and insist that your youngsters explore the great outdoors. The great outdoors of books, of the Internet, of loving and stimulating relationships with family and friends, of trips to libraries and museums—the infinite varieties of life both inside and outside the house.

## THE READING CRISIS

Reading is the bedrock of academic success. Pupils who read on or above grade level probably will perform better in school than those who read below grade level. The more children know about reading, writing, listening, and speaking before they arrive at school, the better prepared they are to become successful readers.

Yet as I said earlier in the Introduction, far too many African-American children struggle with reading. Roughly two out of three black children can barely read by the fourth grade, according to the 2000 National Assessment of Educational Progress (NAEP). Strangely enough, some studies show that earlier when youngsters are four or five years old, they tend to love reading and learning new words. What on earth happens in-between and what can anybody do about it?

Learning to read starts early—and it starts right at home. Keep in mind that literacy is more than just being able to read and write. It is also about talking and vocabulary. It's the ability to understand and communicate information and ideas by others and to others in a clear manner. It's the ability to analyze things and reason your way through issues and situations.

Children are eager to learn, and they achieve when they're raised in home environments and communities that nurture learning. Research shows that:

- Early childhood years, birth to age four, are critical to reading and literacy development.
- Reading aloud to children when they're really young is the single most effective way to help them build the understanding and skills they need to become good readers themselves.
- Children who are exposed to a wide range of words during conversations with adults learn the words they will later need to recognize and understand when they're reading.
- The more children know about reading, writing, listening, and speaking before they arrive at school, the better prepared they are to become successful readers.
- For children whose first language isn't English, a firm grasp of their first language promotes school success in the second language.

Every black parent, caregiver, and leader, every black group and organization, indeed, the entire African-American community, should concentrate on overcoming this crisis in reading and learning. Whether we're parents or grandparents, pastors or mentors, we must make absolutely certain that every child we're responsible for learns to read and write, reason and compute, and navigate the Internet. If your son can read, he can study African history and Western civilization. If your daughter can read, she can absorb the teachings of the Bible and appreciate the writings of authors from Toni Morrison and William Shakespeare, to Bebe Moore Campbell and Stephen King. If your children can't read, all they'll ever learn is what they see on the tube and hear on the streets.

As a youngster, I was obsessed with baseball. There was no doubt in my mind whatsoever that I would become a major league ballplayer. My inability to hit a curveball eventually dashed that dream when I was about 15. Anyway, as a gradeschooler, I read every book and magazine article I could get my hands on about my heroes on the Brooklyn Dodgers and the Cleveland Indians. Why those teams in particular? Because they were the first to bring black players to the major leagues.

My reading skills strengthened rapidly as I worked my way up from children's books to materials written for adults. There wasn't any article about baseball that I couldn't read and understand. I perfected my ability to do long division and decimals by calculating batting averages and pitchers' earned run averages. In fact, mastering how to do these routine baseball statistics helped clarify what those fundamental math procedures really meant.

Each year my elementary school staged a science fair. Every pupil was expected to prepare and display a project. It was a very big deal. The science fair drew a huge and enthusiastic audience of parents, grandparents, church members, and local businesspeople, such as the shopkeepers who sold us all those penny candies that kept dentists in business. Come to think of it, the shopkeepers and dentists might have been in cahoots.

Let's dust off this idea and update it. Imagine how wonderful it would be if a school, a church, or some civic groups would sponsor literacy fairs. Have all the children prepare some project of their choosing that required reading, writing, or spoken performance. They could recite a poem they liked or an essay they had composed. They could perform a dramatic skit. Unlike in my day, however, we don't need to award blue ribbons for first place. Anointing some youngsters as winners means labeling most of them as also-rans or losers. That defeats the whole purpose of mobilizing communities to promote literacy and making sure every child reads. To my way of thinking, every child who submits a presentable piece of work would be viewed as a winner.

"Reading is the key to academic success. It's as simple as that," says Velma Cobb, who before coming to the National Urban League was a reading specialist in the inner-city schools of Roxbury, Massachusetts, and who holds a master's degree in reading from Harvard and a doctorate in educational administration from Columbia University. "Reading allows you to transcend where you are and opens new windows to your world. Getting young children to love reading as early as possible is essential for their doing well and achieving in school."

Dr. Cobb grew up in a poor neighborhood in Cleveland. Neither of her parents was college educated and she is the first Ph.D. in her family. "Reading was always encouraged," she recalls. "I used to hang out at the library where, at first, I didn't read. Then one day I picked up a book and was transformed. Reading allowed me to go where I wanted to go. I could dream about what the book said and go even further in my imagination. I was exposed to a whole new universe, one of infinite possibilities and aspirations."

## INSPIRING THE LOVE OF READING

Although our ability to read and write continues to develop throughout our lifetime, the early childhood years are by far the most important period for laying the foundation for literacy. Educators and experts agree that every child should learn to read well enough by the end of the third grade so that he or she is solidly on course for academic success in all subject areas the rest of the way through school. It's equally important to nurture and help sustain children's interest in reading and writing for their own enjoyment, information, and communication.

Failure to lay this literacy foundation until your children enter kindergarten can severely limit how well they'll ever be able to read and write. But developing the ability to read and write doesn't happen out of the blue like magic. Making sure it happens requires genuine commitment, careful planning, quality instruction—and practice, practice, practice. Use your imagination to turn everyday events into opportunities to learn and to practice. It also helps to make the learning process as much fun as possible.

Listen to how Alexis Gabrielle, a mother and grandmother from Brooklyn, New York, approached her role as her child's—and her grandchild's—first teacher. "At my home, we eat encyclopedias for breakfast and dictionaries for lunch," she laughs. "Just enjoying life isn't enough—you have to enhance your child's educational opportunities at every turn. Even reading signs out loud when you're riding on the bus together and looking out the window. Whenever I used to take my children on trips—and now my grandchildren—I had them write up what they did and make drawings of their experiences. I always cook before we leave, so I can spend time with them on their 'reports' when we get back."

Like many parents, Ms. Gabrielle stimulates an interest in reading in her children and grandchildren through her intuition and common sense. She doesn't possess a graduate degree in literacy development. But I bet the experts agree completely with her that storybooks aren't the only way of exposing children to written language. She knows from real-world experience that children can become better readers by practicing on labels, signs, and other printed things they routinely see around them.

According to the National Association for the Education of Young Children and the International Reading Association, children will initially use what they see as clues to help figure out what something says. Then as they begin to undertand what's in the alphabet and how it works, however, they start putting letters together, translating them into sounds, and connecting this information with a known meaning.

Children need to learn not only the technical skills of reading and writing, but also the tools to sharpen their thinking and reasoning. They must have the opportunity to practice what they've learned about print with other friends and on their own. Even after they enter elementary school, make sure they continue to practice and perfect their reading skills both in the classroom and at home. A terrific resource for parents is the series of *Black Books Galore!* guides to great African-American children's books coauthored by Donna Rand and Toni Trent Parker.

Reading is a skill and an art. It's your responsibility to make sure your children get the proper instruction and guidance and support they need. But that isn't all you're obliged to do if you are raising a child. It's also up to you to inspire and nurture their natural love of learning. You can unleash your children's natural reading potential by:

1. **Encouraging the use of language to express feelings and needs.** A solid command of spoken language increases competency in reading and writing. Keep talking with your children about the things they see and do, like and dislike, and help them express these feelings.

2. **Reading aloud to your child.** Start with bedtime stories. Then, if you have some time before or after dinner, in the morning, or when your children come home from school, share a story or part of one. Use the time when you're traveling or even when you are waiting with them in a doctor's office as a reading opportunity. Keep lots of books in your home—this sends a message to your children that reading is very important to you and that it should be to them as well.

3. **Inspiring the enjoyment of the sound of language.** A child's love of rhymes, chants, and songs seems so natural and inborn. Research confirms this! These ways of "playing" with language really do promote literacy development. So enjoy language with your children. Make up funny-sounding rhymes and silly words. Infants, toddlers, and young children will be learning all the while as they laugh along with you.

4. **Taking them on trips.** When our daughters were in grade school, we used to take them on family excursions on Saturdays and Sundays. Since we didn't have any money to spare, most of the time we didn't venture very far from home. Often this involved a trip to a nearby museum that didn't charge admission. An especially convenient one was Yale University's Peabody Museum in New Haven. It's a pretty old-fashioned museum filled with dusty, dimly lit dinosaur skeletons. Our kids used to complain mildly when we set out that we were headed off on another of those "edumacational" trips where they were expected to learn something instead of playing around. But for all their moaning, those ancient

dinosaur bones never failed to interest them. Plus they got to practice reading the captions next to the skeletons and in the display cases.

Interestingly enough, our middle daughter returned to New Haven nearly twenty years later to attend law school. In her spare time, she mentored some children at a nearby public school. Sometimes they went on excursions together. Three guesses where she took them. Yup! Right back to her old stomping ground—the dusty, trusty Peabody Museum. This confirms one of the basic laws of parenting that I've learned over the years—there's often a delayed reaction when parents do something right. So if your gut tells you that something is the correct thing to do, don't let your children get away with talking you out of it.

5. **Making sure they write as well.** When it's time to compile the weekly shopping list, get your son to help you write it up. The next time your daughter shows you a drawing, ask her to write down what it's about. When youngsters return from a family excursion, have them talk about what they saw and write up what they learned and how they felt about the trip—even if it was boring. Encourage them to write short stories, poems, or songs, or anything else that suits their fancy. Have them talk to you about what they've written so they begin to understand how they can use writing as a way to express their ideas and feelings.

Your children, like all children, are born eager to learn. So from the time they're born, fill your home full of materials and opportunities for them to see, hear, and use both spoken and written language. "We can't start too soon," says T. Willard Fair, president and CEO of the Urban League of Greater Miami. "The major reason our children are not achieving is because we have a reading deficit. Literacy—and especially early literacy—must be our main focus."

## READ AND RISE: WHAT WORKS

Many youngsters read just fine and already are well on their way to academic success in school. Unfortunately that isn't true for two out of three black students and for three out of five Latino and Native American children in the fourth grade. So parents, caregivers, and schools have their work cut out for them to get these youngsters on the right course.

That's the bad news. The good news is we know a lot now about why some youngsters scored well on the national reading exam compared to those who didn't:

- Students who read more in school and for homework scored higher than those students who read less on a daily basis.
- Students who spent an hour to an hour and a half daily on homework scored higher on the reading test than those who spent one hour or less.
- Fourth graders who said they typically write long answers for test questions and assignments that involved reading on a regular basis scored higher than students who rarely did so.
- Students who read for fun every day scored higher than students who said they don't read for leisure very often.

The key is to get your children off on the right foot when it comes to reading so they aren't frustrated later on as school becomes more demanding and reading is key to just about every academic course they'll take all the way through high school. The saying that an ounce of prevention is worth a pound of cure holds true for early literacy as well as health care.

As parents and caregivers, you bear primary responsibility for rearing your child. One of the single most important jobs you have is to make certain your youngster gets a solid foundation in reading and literacy. Don't settle simply for a baby-sitting arrangement or send your child to just any day care center, Head Start or Early Head Start center, or nursery school. Check out whether it has qualified preschool teachers and a bona fide literacy curriculum that prepares the preschoolers to become good readers. Find out from your local school board or social services agency in your area whether the center is officially certified by your city, county, or state. You can also contact one of the ten regional offices of the Administration for Children and Families (ACF), a federal agency that oversees Head Start and other programs relating to children and families. To find the ACF regional office closest to you, check out the agency's website at www.acf.dhhs.gov. If the center isn't certified, then look elsewhere. Insist on seeing the center's statistics on how well its young graduates fare once they arrive in kindergarten.

Parents have a huge role to play here. There are plenty of very practical things you can do to help your youngster become a good reader. Believe me, it isn't rocket science. The key is to make a solemn vow—to yourself and, most important, to your child—that you're going to do whatever it takes.

In 2001, the National Urban League teamed up with Scholastic Inc. to produce a guide for parents and caregivers called *Read and Rise: Preparing Our Children for a Lifetime of Success*. It's chockfull of practical and proven tips on how to help your child become a good reader. Scholastic knows this subject cold. After all, it's the world's largest publisher and distributor of children's books. Tens of millions of schoolchildren have experienced the joys of reading and discovery through *Scholastic Magazine* over the years.

This clear and easy-to-use booklet lays out the kinds of things parents and caregivers can do every step of the way. It lays out literacy-building activities you can do with your children even before they've learned to read. It explains the reading development skills that youngsters should practice at a particular age. The guide outlines what parents can do with their children at home to encourage them to read on their own.

In other words, *Read and Rise* recommends activities for when your kids are infants and toddlers and then when they reach preschool age. It goes on to suggest what you should do when they are in kindergarten, first grade, second grade, and third grade. As you can imagine, different ages require different methods and present different opportunities. After all, the academic demands of school grow as your child gets older.

I have already mentioned some of the tips that are contained in *Read and Rise*. It's tempting to repeat all of them right here while your attention is focused on how to help your children become good readers right from the beginning. But the guide is very comprehensive, and covering all the tips would take up too much space in this section of the book.

So I've done the next best thing. Since the National Urban League and Scholastic Inc. are deeply committed to doing whatever they can to promote early literacy and reading, they've graciously granted permission to reprint the entire guide at the very end of this book. You'll find *Read and Rise* in Appendix A at the back of this book.

The strong interest in this guide right from the start shows how eager parents are for helpful information. More than half a million copies of *Read and Rise* were distributed within months after it was released. Scholastic and local Urban Leagues across the country provided it to parents and caregivers free of charge through PTAs, churches, barbershops, beauty parlors, community centers, and neighborhood stores and shops. The complete guide is also available online at the National Urban League's website at www.nul.org/readandrise and on Scholastic's website at www.scholastic.com/readandrise.

"When parents and communities are equipped with information, tools, and resources, there's no limit to what our children can achieve," says Dick Robinson, the president and CEO of Scholastic. "And significant change often comes through grassroots efforts."

Sarah Murdoch is the assistant director of the Reach Out and Read early literacy program at Bellevue Hospital Center, the largest public hospital in New York City. A national hospital-based effort, Reach Out and Read counts on volunteers to read aloud to children between the ages of nine months and five years who are waiting to be seen at busy medical clinics that serve needy patients free of charge. After the examination, the doctor presents the child with a brand new book as part of the visit.

"The kids are thrilled, the parents surprised, and the doctors are really pleased," Ms. Murdoch says. "We tell the parents that a book is just as important as an immunization because it's their child's future, their life, their hope. What better prescription can you give a child?"

Ms. Murdoch explains that the program is considering including babies younger than nine months because they respond so eagerly to the spoken word. "The kids love the comfort of hearing a human voice instead of the television, and they adore the contact," she says. "They snuggle up to the reader, and listen attentively to the stories. What's really wonderful is to see when they are able to begin reading themselves. There's an excitement and anticipation as the printed word unfolds. You see them reading to their younger siblings—proud as punch to be able to communicate their love of learning to a gurgling month-old brother or a very impressed three-year-old sister."

While I don't want to flood you with the opinions of experts, it's really a mistake to ignore or overlook what some of them have to say. Take Mem Fox, a literary expert, who is the author of *Reading Magic: Why Reading Aloud to Our Children Will Change Their Lives Forever*. Every adult who is rearing a child needs to hear Ms. Fox's message loud and clear—and then heed it. As a favor to yourself and especially to your children, please be sure you pause long enough here to make certain her point really sinks in.

According to Ms. Fox, only about a quarter of the human brain's potential is developed before birth. Most brain development happens during the first three years of life, and especially by the time a child turns one year old. Ninety percent of the brain is actually formed by age three.

Ms. Fox goes on to say that the connections in a child's brain that determine how creative, imaginative, and clever the child will become have already been "wired" by the time a child turns one. "Children who come to school without any experience of books or stories, poems, or rhymes take years to learn to read, and a few never learn at all," she writes. "Reading aloud from birth to twelve months makes a child clever!"

## THE CHURCH AND EARLY LITERACY

In the heyday of the civil rights struggles of the 1950s and 1960s, the black church was the engine that propelled the movement forward. It supplied much of the leadership, many of the sergeants, and most of the foot soldiers. The truth is that without the church to provide the spiritual guidance, the momentum, and the manpower, there probably wouldn't have been a civil rights movement. At a minimum, the progress that was made would have taken decades longer. Nor were African-American churches the only religious institutions involved. The pastors and congregations from synagogues and Catholic churches, Unitarian and Episcopalian churches were pivotal players in the drama.

Education is the civil rights challenge of the twenty-first century. Unless poor and minority children are well educated, they are destined for economic apartheid. They'll live out their lives as "have-nots" instead of "haves." Race discrimination lives on in the labor markets and criminal justice system of this country, and it must be fought wherever it rears its ugly head. But children who aren't prepared academically have little chance of getting ahead economically.

That's why it's so important for churches to take up the literacy challenge with the same zeal and single-mindedness they devoted to the civil rights struggles of days gone by. Our children desperately need for the churches to mobilize our communities around literacy and achievement. Every churchgoing parent and caregiver should band together with other members to persuade their pastor and their church into the fray. Just think of all those active and retired educators in the church congregations who could be pressed into service and who probably would relish the assignment.

Churches can move mountains—in our spirits, our hearts, and our communities—when they really set their minds to it. We must not allow an institution as important as the church to be missing in action on an issue as important as literacy.

Imagination is the only limit on what churches could do if they took this on. In the world of black churches, there are eight national Protestant denominations, two Muslim denominations, and plenty of Catholic churches that serve our communities. That doesn't even include those churches that aren't formally affiliated with national denominations or, in many cases, those massive megachurches that are sprouting up in communities all across the country.

Just think of what these national denominations could do to help ensure that the children in their flocks become good readers and high achievers. For starters, the national leaders of the denominations could declare that it's the business of that denomination and thus every member church to make certain that each and every child learns to read on grade or better by the fourth grade, and preferably sooner. Taking a cue from the parents' guide that the National Urban League and Scholastic Inc. created, each denomination could form a *Read and Rise* Network. The Network would sponsor dialogues among churches around reading and literacy issues and promotion. It also could: (1) help connect churches with local community literacy resources and organizations; and (2) help promote best early literacy practices at church-run preschool, child care/day care, and school programs.

Of course, the real action is on the ground, in communities where children live and in churches where they worship. I could see parents and caregivers getting their own churches involved in three ways at least. To begin with, individual churches could mount a concerted effort to make certain that every child affiliated with that church becomes a good reader and performs at grade level or better by the fourth grade. Second, each church could undertake activities that promote a culture of literacy at the church and in the surrounding community. Third, church leaders can work with and pressure local schools to make certain they are doing their level best to ensure that children enrolled there become good readers.

Let's begin with the children in the church itself. I could see the pastor and the members of the church doing all manner of things that would definitely make a difference. The pastor could set the overall tone by preaching and teaching from the pulpit about the critical importance of reading and the essential role that reading plays in the social, economic, and spiritual development of young people and their families when they become adults. In sermons and messages, the pastor would inform the congregation about the clear link between literacy, employability, and economic well-being. On the other hand, they'd also be told about the connection between low levels of literacy and such social ills as unemployment, under-employment, delinquency, and incarceration. Of course, the pastor should urge parents and caregivers in the church to take an active and engaged role in their children's reading and literacy develop-ment. And tell relatives and friends they should pitch in if parents need help or aren't up to what's required.

The church wouldn't stop there if I had my way. I'd love for the pastor to declare that it's the intention of the church to see to it that *every* child in the congregation becomes a proficient reader. Then mobilize parents, other members, and groups in the church to make it happen. For instance, one of the groups in the church could host a *Read and Rise* family night. It could also enlist the help of educa-tors within the church family, the local Urban League affiliate, the library, or other literacy-oriented organizations to host a "basic training" session on the principles and practices featured in the *Read and Rise* guide. Each family that attends would leave with a new children's book to take home. This event also can be opened up to the community at large as an outreach activity of the church.

That's just for starters. If the church really got serious, the pastor would secure a firm commitment from each parent and caregiver actually to do the activities recommended in the guide over an agreed-upon period of weeks and have them report back on whether they have fulfilled their pledge. From there, a cadre of volunteers from the church would be created, men and women who are avail-able to advise and assist parents who want to do the right thing but, perhaps because of their own insecurities or literacy challenges, find the advice in the guide too difficult to follow. For instance, these volunteers could read to children on story-telling afternoons or nights, and have the children read to the volunteers along with the parents when they come of age. If I was the pastor, I'd even have parents bring their youngsters' report cards to church so that I, or a deaconess or deacon, could check on whether they are reading at grade level, and assist the parents in intervening at school if need be.

Lastly, I could see the church launching a book club for children or entire families. Different children's books might be featured each month and families would be encouraged to meet to read and discuss them on a regular basis. This could be promoted as a whole family activity. The point is to make sure the church thinks of itself as and becomes known as a "reading" congregation.

In addition to its work with individual children and families, the church could sponsor lots of activities aimed at fostering reading and literacy throughout the church and surrounding neighborhood. Many religious organizations run preschool programs. Some are top flight, with all the latest literacy ideas. Others basically are baby-sitting services. That's convenient for the parents, but hardly good enough for the children in this day and age when it's so important for them to start school fully prepared to read.

So every church should see to it that any preschool, child care, or K–12 schools they run meet rigorous standards and best practices for early learning, reading, and literacy. These programs should have adequate reading/literacy development resources, including recommended books and materials, not to mention fully qualified staff. The idea is to ensure that the church's child-centered programs—whether they're baby-sitting services, before-care, or after-school programs—promote the value of reading and have the necessary educational resources to support these literacy efforts.

Above all, churches should show children that reading is fun and learning is delightful. They can arrange for trips to the local library, for example. One idea I especially like is for churches to organize or co-sponsor a literacy fair at the church or in the neighborhood. Children from the church and the community would do a literacy project—such as reading a book, writing an essay, or performing a play—and then present their work on the day of the fair in front of parents and well-wishers who attend. Children's books and reading materials could also be sold at the fair.

Pastors who get the message, and who have ready access to radio and television, can use the media to promote the literacy message and tell their listeners how to get hold of the *Read and Rise* guide. Individual churches can make the guide available to the community as an outreach initiative. Church members of all ages could be encouraged to volunteer as reading tutors in the church itself, with local schools that welcome volunteers, and with libraries and other community-based reading and literacy organizations that offer tutoring.

One of the biggest stumbling blocks for literacy achievement for many children, particularly low-income children, is a lack of access to books and reading materials. Far too many children are growing up with few, if any, books and reading materials in their lives. In response to this need, I could see churches staging community book drives to collect books for local literacy organizations or to help build church "reading zones."

Finally, parents and caregivers often hit a wall when they try to work with their children's schools and persuade these schools to improve. Here's where church leaders need to step in on behalf of their members and their neighbors. Just as ministers were right there in the forefront of the civil rights movement, I believe they should be on the front line in advocating for better schools. They should be well informed about the performance of local schools in ensuring that children read well. If large numbers of students routinely fall short, then church and community leaders should meet with school district officials to determine what corrective action they intend to take, and whether the district intends to learn from other school systems that have successfully raised the reading levels of children.

A collaborative approach may produce results. If it doesn't, however, and the children continue to lag behind, then the community leaders and ministers should up the ante by mobilizing parents and community people to install a new school board and superintendent who understand the need for change. As I describe elsewhere in this book, that's exactly what happened in Mount Vernon, New York, an urbanized suburb just north of New York City. What a wonderful difference that made in the lives and life prospects of

the children of that school district. All because some leading ministers and heads of civic groups like the Urban League cared passion-
ately enough to get involved and insist on change. As a powerful
engine of positive change, the church can do for literacy what it did
for civil rights.

## WHAT ELSE YOU CAN DO

Reading is the cornerstone of learning, and every parent and
caregiver is responsible for making certain their child gets a solid
education. I believe that when a mother and father bring a baby
into this world, they relinquish any right to offer excuses for failing
to make certain their offspring gets an education.

Saying that you're too impoverished, too poorly educated, or
too overburdened yourself doesn't wash in my opinion. If life is too
much of a struggle or, frankly, if your own reading skills are too
weak to be of much use in supporting your child, don't be defeated.
Seek help from a relative or friend. Ask at your church whether
there's a retired schoolteacher, postal worker, or secretary who can
pitch in. The bottom line is don't stop until you find somebody
who's willing to spend some time with you and your child doing the
kinds of activities that boost literacy skills. Come to think of it, if
reading doesn't come easily, you could benefit as well.

I know that America hasn't gotten rid of racism and discrimination everywhere in the land. I know that many public schools don't
educate minority children nearly as well as they should. But I beg
you. Please don't use racism as a reason why you won't do your
level best to make sure your child becomes a good reader. As the
slogan in that Nike television commercial says, "Just do it." Your
children's future depends on whether you are willing to do all you
can do to help them, to paraphrase that Army slogan, "Be all they
can be."

As parents and caregivers, you set the family priorities and the
tone at home. You can make reading important to your children by

showing them that it's hugely important to you. One of the key factors contributing to scholastic success of the Meyerhoff scholars interviewed in *Beating the Odds: Raising Academically Successful African American Males* was reading, beginning with parents who read to their children at a young age.

"When my son was born, my wife and I were avid readers," one father says. "The big thing for him was getting his own library card when he was five. He had his name on the card and felt like a big shot. We read to him all the time, so he knew his ABCs by the time he started school. Parents must do this before school because teachers cannot do everything."

Almost all of the Meyerhoff scholars reported that their mothers read to them when they were young. Just over half of them said their fathers did as well. These determined parents did most of the things I've already mentioned to promote reading by their sons and daughters. They also advise other parents to:

- Encourage children to read anything, from baseball cards to comic books, as I did.
- Have books on tape available.
- Name objects when children point to them. (One mother remembers saying, "Yes, that is a green leaf," in order to name the object and teach the color.)
- Avoid becoming addicted to the tube. Three-quarters of parents said that reading was more important than television watching in their family.

Delores is a high school history teacher in Richmond, Virginia, and the mother of three teenagers. "I grew up without a television in my house—on purpose," she says. "My parents wouldn't allow it, and although I used to go to my friends' houses to catch a favorite program when I could, I grew up reading. It was that or doing nothing! My favorite books were biographies of African-American achievers who matured in the 1940s and 1950s; I found them to be inspiring and used them as role models.

"I guess you can say I followed my parents' example," Delores goes on. "I never had a TV in our house, and although my children complained—more loudly than I remember doing!—they were forced to develop other interests to take up their time. My daughter got into music, then ballet. My son joined the science club at his school and spent a lot of time there. He's now sixteen and just won a prize in a NASA contest. We do listen to a lot of radio, but it's more like background noise, not a primary activity."

Television, computer games, and the Internet are all part of modern-day life. Most of us have such diversions—and in some cases, necessities—in our homes. We probably rely on them and enjoy them as much as our children. But it is our job to make books a big part of our children's lives, too. Not just for their instructional value, but also as a source of pure entertainment. Books can be friendly and enthusiastic tour guides to the world that lies beyond your child's bedroom.

"If children are raised in a house that values reading, they will also respect it," says LaVerne Bloomfield-Jiles, project manager of the Standard Keepers program of the New York Urban League. "Children learn what they live. Yet before parents become involved, they must be informed. The more we know, the more we can help our kids. And nothing is more important than being able to read and treasure the printed word."

A first love is seldom forgotten. Once a child falls in love with books, that infatuation lasts forever. Emma M. Talbott, the author of *The Joy and Challenge of Raising African American Children*, has devised a wonderful "Ten-Point Plan to Cultivate a Love of Reading in Your Children." Here's what she recommends:

1. Select a book suited to the interest and age of your child.
2. Sit close to the child or let him sit in your lap.
3. If the child wishes, let her hold the book.
4. Read with expression and enthusiasm. Your reading voice should sound very much like your regular speaking voice.
5. Point to the words that you are reading.

6. Stop frequently and talk about the pictures.
7. Be relaxed. Avoid rushing through the book.
8. Help your child relate to events in the story in a personal way.
9. After you have finished reading, discuss the story/book.
10. Children usually have a favorite book. Be willing to reread it many times.

Ms. Talbott got it exactly right as far as I'm concerned. That's certainly the way it was with our daughters. I'll never forget—nor have they ever forgotten—how they used to snuggle up next to my wife and me in their beds and how we read *Winnie the Pooh* and *The Cat in the Hat* to them over and over and over. They could never get enough of these stories. My wife and I were like a tag team in wrestling. We'd rotate nights reading to them. That way we never got weary. More important, our children understood that reading was a "Mommy thing" *and* a "Daddy thing," and therefore that reading to them and with them was a big deal to both of us.

It's important for children to see reading role models at home. Fill your house with all kinds of reading materials—the Holy Bible, books, magazines, newspapers, and so on. Studies show that children who are surrounded by lots of reading matter at home tend to read better than those who aren't exposed to it.

Reading aloud to your children helps build the knowledge and skills they need to become good readers. And talk to them a lot as well. Children who listen to a wide range of words during conversations with adults gradually learn the words that they'll need to recognize and understand later on when reading.

Reading should be a family priority right from the day your child emerges from the womb. Next to the gifts of life and of love, literacy is the grandest and most enduring present parents can bestow on children because it nurtures their minds, expands their horizons, and unleashes their potential.

# KEY READING SKILLS

As a parent or caregiver, you need to keep close track of whether your child is acquiring the right literacy skills at the right pace. You should also keep an eagle eye out for any telltale sign that your youngster is slipping behind. Right now you are probably asking: "How on earth am I supposed to figure that out if I'm not a teacher?" Obviously, most folks raising children aren't educators.

Fortunately, two organizations that are expert on this subject have outlined some benchmarks for appraising whether your child is making the right amount of progress grade by grade. These groups are the National Association for the Education of Young Children and the International Reading Association. These benchmarks will help you gauge your child's reading skills and potential.

Your infant and toddler (ages birth to 2) should:

- Communicate first with gestures and expressions, then with simple sounds and words.
- Enjoy listening to stories, songs, and rhymes.
- Love hearing the same sounds and stories over and over and over.
- Start using language to ask questions and express feelings and ideas.

The more words your children hear by age 2, the larger their vocabulary. Surround them with face-to-face interactions and lots of talking—lean into their crib, coo to them, play "peek-a-boo," sing a song or lullaby, read a story, or just respond to their coos, laughs, and cries.

In preschool (ages 3–4), your child should:

- Enjoy asking a lot of questions and talking about everything.
- Like listening to and discussing storybooks.
- Understand that print carries a message.
- Begin attempting to read and write.
- Identify labels and signs in their surroundings.

• Use known letters or approximations of letters to represent written language, especially meaningful words like their name and phrases such as "I love you."

Reading aloud with your children for as little as fifteen minutes a day will help them become better readers. They will learn how print "works" by holding a book, turning the pages, listening carefully, and enjoying a story. It's important to choose books that reflect your children's culture, home, identity, and language.

In kindergarten (ages 5–6), your child should:

• Enjoy being read to and be able to retell simple stories or informational texts.
• "Read" familiar books alone, often by memory.
• Use language to explain and explore.
• Begin to write letters of the alphabet and some frequently used words, such as their own name (first and last), as well as "the," "mom," "dad," "and," "I," "my."
• Use descriptive language to explain and explore things and ideas.
• Recognize letters and sounds that are similar to one another.
• Recognize rhymes and words and pictures that begin with the same sound.
• Understand left-to-right and top-to-bottom.
• Be able to match spoken words with written ones.

This is the age when your children should join the local library. Take them there on a regular basis and help them choose books they will like. The library is a magical place for young children, a private and quiet space where they can learn about new worlds and begin to dream their own dreams.

In first grade (ages 6–7), your child should:

• Read and retell familiar stories.
• Use strategies—such as rereading, predicting, and questioning—when they are puzzled by something they read.

- Read and write for fun and for other purely personal reasons when they feel like it.
- Read aloud with reasonable accuracy and relative ease.
- Be able to identify new words based on the sounds of letters, parts of words, and the context in which the word is used.
- Identify an increasing number of words by sight.
- Say most of the sounds in spelling a word.
- Begin using some punctuation and capitalization.

Parents of first-graders should provide children with opportunities to read a variety of books and magazines so they can practice their newfound skills. It's also time to start mixing up your reading routine with them. One day read to your child; the next day read with your child. Then simply listen as your child reads to you.

In second grade (ages 7–8), your child should:

- Enjoy reading fiction and nonfiction books.
- Show signs of a growing vocabulary.
- Read with greater accuracy and ease.
- Use familiar patterns of letters and relationships of sounds to spell words.
- Punctuate simple sentences correctly and check their writing for errors.
- Identify more and more words by sight.
- Write about a variety of topics for various audiences.
- Read every day and use reading to research topics.

That isn't all you should do for them at this age. Help your children gain confidence in their reading and writing ability by praising them often. Allow them to pick their own books. Correct their errors when they ask for help, but don't correct them so often or so critically that they start losing confidence in themselves. If they become bored with a book, let them take a breather. Lastly, if you have any concerns about your child's reading ability at this stage, raise them with their teacher and figure out together how to get your child back on track as quickly as possible.

In third grade (ages 8–9), your child should:

- Read fluently and enjoy reading.
- Have a pretty extensive and expanding vocabulary.
- Attempt different types of writing, such as stories, reports, and poems.
- Spell more words correctly by seeing how words look and using spelling rules.
- Know how to figure out the meaning of unfamiliar words.
- Edit and revise their own writing.

There's even more you should do to encourage your young readers. For instance, create a space in your home where they can comfortably read and write, and where they can stash their books and reference materials. As they move through grade school, continue to keep close tabs on their progress and stay in close touch with their teachers. For reasons that aren't entirely clear, some African-American boys start sloughing off academically around the third grade. Monitor their performance regularly and step in quickly if they stop moving forward as they should.

And remember—don't be in a rush to stop reading to them and with them. No matter what age your children are, continue to read to them and have them read aloud to you. I'm talking not only about school assignments all the time. Any topic that interests either of you will do the trick. Reading aloud increases vocabulary and comprehension through listening. It strengthens the loving bond between parent and child because reading together is a cozy and enjoyable experience.

As I said earlier, reading is the bedrock of academic success. *The Preparation Gap* will evaporate like dew on a summer's day if parents and caregivers make absolutely certain their youngsters become good readers.

# CHAPTER FOUR

## High Achievement Starts at Home

By now, some readers might be saying to themselves that I've got some nerve offering advice about how to help your children become achievers in light of the fact that I got high grades all the way through school. What do I know, you may be wondering, about struggling to overcome odds and striving to excel? Believe me, it didn't happen automatically. It took loads of effort to make academics come easily. I worked really hard at doing well. To get the excellent grades I earned, I paid close attention in class and completed most every homework assignment that my teachers handed out. I didn't skip class or play hooky from school.

Another big reason I got good grades is that my parents stood behind me every step of the way. They expected me to succeed and were always there with soothing words of encouragement or wise advice just when I needed it. No matter how busy my father was or what his office hours were, he never missed a school assembly where I received an academic award. He was a pretty reserved man most of the time. But right at that moment when some honor was conferred on me, he'd let out a proud hoot of joy. That way I always knew he was sharing that special moment with me.

Let me give you another example of what a crucial difference parents can make. The summer of 1958 between my eleventh and twelfth grades, I was selected for a highly competitive internship with a U.S. Defense Department subcontractor known as the Operations Research Office (ORO). The students who were chosen had to excel in math and science. I more than cleared that hurdle. In fact, I was the first black student ever selected for the program.

Mind you, this was the height of the Cold War in the late 1950s. For our assignment that summer, we calculated the damage that would likely be done if Russia or China dropped a hydrogen bomb on a major American city. The point of our study was to estimate how much investment in civil defense would be required to minimize the physical devastation and loss of human life.

That was fine. But the busybodies at ORO also took it upon themselves to give the interns a battery of tests designed to measure our ability and project our potential. Keep in mind that we'd already shown we were strong students by winning the coveted internships in the first place. You couldn't be chosen otherwise. While my verbal SATs were in the high 500s, if I recall correctly, I'd scored somewhere in the 700s in math, for a cumulative score in the high 1300s. Not shabby at all, and unquestionably smack inside the bull's-eye for admission to Ivy League colleges and other selective institutions of higher learning.

I shall never, ever in life, forget the appraisal of my life prospects that ORO gave me when they informed me of the test results. "You probably will get to go to college," they reassured me. Yet in the next breath they dropped a bombshell that still echoes in my ears decades later. ORO's testing expert told me: "But you should not count on getting into graduate or professional school."

Stunned and furious, I walked, silently steaming, out of the room. When I got home that night, I reported that encounter to my parents. To their everlasting credit, they had the good sense and confidence in me to tell me to pay those test results absolutely no mind. Instead of getting discouraged, I became even more determined to succeed just to show ORO how wrong they'd been about me.

I still remember how badly they misread me as though it happened yesterday. I recalled it in 1963 when I earned my B.A. degree from Amherst College, one of the truly great and most selective colleges in this country. I remembered it when my proud parents watched me march across the stage three years later to receive my law degree from Yale, which year after year is ranked the best law school in the nation.

I remembered it when I received the Medal of Honor from Yale Law School, a prized honor that had also been bestowed on former presidents of the United States. And I reflected on what ORO said about me when I earned an honorary degree from Amherst in 1998 and another from Yale in 2000.

I recount these honors not to toot my own horn but to show how the experience with ORO made me deeply mistrustful early on about the ability of standardized exams to predict how well someone will do in school and in life. More important, I learned how dangerous these exam scores can be in the hands of people who are skeptical of your potential or actually mean you harm. It's experiences like mine that make African Americans and other traditional targets of discrimination so suspicious of high-stakes exams that are used to determine who will get through the gates of opportunity.

By my senior year of high school, I ranked tenth in my class of roughly 700 students thanks to my stellar grades, which included only three or four B's during the entire time there. So I set my sights on the very best colleges east of the Mississippi. By the way, my high school was all-white prior to the U.S. Supreme Court decree in 1954 that ended racial segregation. In the fall of my senior year, I paid the obligatory visit to my guidance counselor. She was a holdover from the old days who was known for giving black students a hard time.

I asked the guidance counselor where she thought I should apply based on my strong scholastic record. In another of those conversations I'll never forget, she suggested that I apply to some colleges that I knew were several notches below where I should be aiming based on my grades and SAT scores. It was obvious she didn't have my best interests at heart. Fortunately I had the presence of mind to respond that I didn't really need advice like that, and that my parents would help me with the application process from that point forward.

Misleading or malicious advice like this isn't unusual in the black experience. When our eldest daughter was applying to college in 1981, she, too, had compiled a strong academic record that clearly qualified her for America's top colleges and universities. When one of her teachers learned that she intended to apply to Harvard, the teacher tried to steer her elsewhere with the caution that she might not want to work as hard as would be required to graduate from Harvard.

When our daughter recounted this conversation later that night in our kitchen, I just about blew a gasket. It conjured up memories of that encounter with my guidance counselor years ago. I told our daughter to ignore that caution. I didn't want teachers, whose motives I wasn't certain of, telling my kids to trim their sails. Besides, I said, what her teacher evidently didn't know was that the hardest part was getting into Harvard, not getting through it.

Scholastic achievement doesn't just happen like magic. Nor is it a matter of luck. It takes hard work. The desire and motivation to do well stems from a respect for learning and succeeding that's instilled in children by their parents and caregivers. As concerned adults, we must keep in mind that what we do in our homes can be just as critical as any formal classroom situation, perhaps even more so. It is our obligation, it is our duty, to do everything in our power to teach our children to value education and excel in school so that they are fully equipped for citizenship and for self-reliance.

## PARENTAL SUPPORT

Since my parents were college-educated, some people might be inclined to say that academic success was second nature to the Price family. Yes and no. It was expected in our household, that's true. But parents don't need much formal education to understand how vital it is for their children to achieve in school. The illiterate slaves set free by the Emancipation Proclamation got it from the very beginning and pressed their youngsters to get lots of "book learning." My grandparents weren't college grads, but they instilled in my parents a desire to climb higher than they had. Plenty of today's parents get the point even though they're barely educated themselves.

Take the noted African-American pediatric neurosurgeon, Dr. Ben Carson. In his inspiring autobiography, *Gifted Hands,* he recalls how when he was growing up, his illiterate mother had him read aloud to her every night and how much joy that gave him. Although his mother never had a formal education, Dr. Carson was deeply influenced by her respect for the written word and her fierce belief in the power of knowledge.

The most influential role models for young people are adults who respect and revere education. As parents and caregivers, we must create a home environment that nurtures a desire to learn, and that encourages and rewards academic achievement. Even though most of us face the constant challenge of balancing work and family demands, it's a myth that only nonworking parents or those with plenty of time and resources can help their children learn to do well in school. A study published in the *American Educational Research Journal* found that having a supportive adult who helps a child learn and develop skills after school definitely makes a difference, *even if the adult has no formal training in how to help a child.*

That's why, regardless of how much education we have or how much money we make, every one of us is capable of giving our children the support and the skills to become successful students. They say ignorance is no excuse for breaking the law. When it comes to academic success, undereducated, overworked, and apathetic parents are no excuse for youngsters doing poorly in school. It just doesn't have to be. What's required is the fierce determination displayed by those slaves as soon as they were freed, and by resolute parents like Dr. Carson's mother.

"Coming home from school every day marks not the end of but a continuation of what transpired in the classroom," writes Emma M. Talbott in *The Joy and Challenge of Raising African American Children*. "If you are committed to your child's education, you must be willing to give of your time in the home and community by helping create a learning environment independent of what happens at school."

So, how should we go about convincing our children that achievement matters? To Yvette, a mother of four who works full-time managing a law office in suburban Chicago, the answer is very straightforward. "We must meet peer pressure with parental pressure," she says. "From the time our children are born, we must educate them. We can't rely on school alone, but use any and all resources that we have. Recreation, for example, should also be used for discipline and responsibility, especially for African Americans."

Yvette continues: "We must surround our children with books and, if we can't afford books, take our children to the library on a regular basis. We should teach our young people new words and vocabulary, and plan long trips together where they can see different worlds outside their own surroundings. Everything should be geared to their academic achievement—if necessary, tell your children that their education will be good training for them to be on 'Jeopardy' or 'How to Be a Millionaire,' so they can buy their mama a house!"

Parents with college degrees and money aren't the only ones who have what it takes to create a home life that encourages high academic achievement. Not by a long shot. Experts agree that children whose parents create a home environment that encourages learning and who get really involved in their children's education from preschool through elementary school actually earn higher grades than youngsters whose parents aren't involved. The 2000 NAEP report shows beyond a shadow of doubt that parental involvement—both in school and at home—contributes in a big way to a child's academic success. According to the report, "Learning is not limited to the classroom but is a process that continues in, and is shaped by, home environments and social interactions." To be more specific:

- Fourth-graders who regularly discuss their studies with their parents score higher on the NAEP exams than students who rarely talk about it with their folks.
- Students who talk about reading with their family and friends on a weekly basis score higher than those who seldom talk about reading with their family.
- A strong predictor of high achievement is a home filled with reading material, family conversation, educational games, and writing activities that allow children to practice reading skills and master the written word. Students who have access to an array of reading materials in their homes, including books, magazines, newspapers, and encyclopedias, score higher than those who don't.

None of us is born knowing the best way to help our children academically. It's something we learn from our own parents, relatives, teachers, and role models. Effective parents and caregivers add a heavy dose of common sense acquired just by living in the real world.

Steven Layne is the father of two girls, Lynee, 15, and Stephanie, 14. Both are Student Achievers sponsored by the New York Urban League. A former New York City police officer, Mr. Layne believes that the time and energy he and his wife Kathlyn devote to their children really make a difference in their daughters' academic success. Even so, he's the first to confess that participation didn't come easy for him, and that his growing involvement in his daughters' schooling is as much an education for him as it is for them.

"I grew up on Long Island, and even though education was emphasized in my home," Mr. Layne says, "I have to admit that I was somewhat of a knucklehead. I was a jokester and prankster, and just barely got by. What saved me was that I knew from an early age that I wanted to be a police officer and that, to become one, I would have to go to college. I used my goal to focus myself.

"I remember the moment I changed and became serious about getting an education. It was the summer between the ninth and tenth grade, and I was staying with my grandmother, who lived in Harlem on Lenox Avenue and 137th Street. Those days you could stay at the Apollo Theater all day for a single price of admission and see all the shows. I remember walking by the Apollo and looking up. I saw a man staring out the window. Six hours later on my way home, I saw the same man staring out the same window of the theater.

"This was my 'Aha' moment, the one that Oprah talks about. I thought to myself, 'Is that the way I want to end up? Spending my whole day doing nothing and just hanging out?' Of course, now that I think about it, the man might have been working there, but it didn't matter to me at the time. I took one look at him and knew that I wanted to do something with my life.

"I started avoiding my old friends and making new friends. I also sought out mentors who really helped me focus on my studies," Steven Layne continues. "I graduated college, achieved my goal, and became a New York City police officer. When my daughters were born, I saw that in the same way I had to learn to become a police officer, I had to learn how to be a parent. I saw that if your daughters don't get their love from their fathers and mothers, they will get it from somewhere else. I wanted to do right by my daughters, and in order to do so, I knew I had to learn to soften up and hear other opinions and sides to the story. I looked to my church for spiritual guidance and began reading the Bible. I identified with how Jesus acted compassionately and affectionately, yet strongly, and this helped me immensely.

"I used to be with Highway Patrol, and I really loved it. But I changed assignments so I could have more regular hours and be able to be there for my girls. Dinnertime is very important for our family because we all discuss with each other what we did that day. With my new responsibilities, I was able to share that important time of the day with my family on a more regular basis.

"I encourage my daughters to speak freely. I tell them that they have a right to express themselves and say what they want, as long as they're respectful. My wife and I give them three rules: Respect adults, respect yourself, and strive for academic achievement.

"When my wife and I decided to buy a house, my mother advised us to check out the math and reading scores in the school district where the house was located. We did just that and bought a house in a good school district in Staten Island. In this way, we were not only investing in our home, but also investing in our daughters' future. I am so proud of their dedication to their schoolwork—even though they're far above me in many of their studies! Education is the best gift I can give them because it will provide options and opportunities throughout their lives.

"I want my daughters to be exposed to as many new experiences and different kinds of people as possible. I think it's important to take them out of the neighborhood and show them how other people live and work. Above all, they need to see that they have choices and there are all different kinds of people and places out there. I remember when I was sixteen and went to Washington, D.C., for the first time. I thought the people and even the cars would be different than those in New York!

"When I was growing up, I was taught that as a black man I must excel above all. I still believe that African-Americans boys are more greatly challenged than girls, but girls also have to prove their excellence. And if our kids fall between the cracks, believe me it won't be a sidewalk crack but a hole made from a crater. I know from working as a police officer how the streets can take our young people. You have to talk to your children, praise them often, and make your home an open environment. We are our children's buffers and protection against a world that is often confusing and threatening.

"My wife and I are lucky that we are a two-parent household," Mr. Layne concludes. "I see single parents sacrificing a lot for their kids. They should look for any kind of support they can, including other parents, teachers, and mentors. I heed the concept that our family is our community and our community is our family."

This savvy ex-cop clearly knows from firsthand experience on the educational front lines that parents and caregivers hold the key to convincing their children that achievement matters, and for holding the schools they attend accountable for delivering the high-quality education their youngsters deserve.

## WHY THE EARLY YEARS MATTER

Every parent has a gut instinct why the early years in children's lives are vitally important to their development. Mothers probably explain this to their pregnant daughters. I can't speak for fathers, though. Many of us are clueless, at least until we're face to face with our offspring. Then we realize we'd better study up on child development, or at least start listening more closely to our mothers-in-law.

Interestingly enough, when it comes to this topic, human instinct and scientific research agree entirely. As I mentioned earlier, the prestigious Carnegie Task Force laid out why the early years of a child's life matter so much. But it's not only a good preschool or first-rate child care program that prepares a youngster properly for school; according to the Carnegie experts, what happens at home is just as important. Children who are raised in homes that encourage learning and whose parents stay involved in their education at least through the end of elementary school earn higher grades than children whose parents aren't involved.

Elementary school is also the time in children's lives when schools start deciding who has the "goods" to take challenging courses, and who doesn't. This is what's called "tracking" and it's commonplace in the schools, starting around the third grade. The Carnegie Task Force came up with another name for it. They said the early elementary grades are the years of the "big sort," when ability grouping begins in earnest. How children do later on in school depends heavily on where they are routed early on. If they perform well and are placed in a challenging track, that's fine. But if they're routed into special education, watch out. That's definitely the wrong side of the tracks and it should be avoided if at all possible. Once your child is referred to special education, it's difficult to "escape" back into so-called "mainstream" classes. Yet the fact is that plenty of youngsters who are ticketed for special ed actually could survive and succeed in regular classes if they received abundant doses of appropriate instruction and support by teachers who genuinely believe in them.

Maggie Comer didn't need any expert to tell her why the home environment matters so much in the early years. She never served on a big-deal foundation task force. The only Ph.D. she possessed was in common sense. But her words, remembered by her son, Dr. James Comer, in his moving book entitled *Maggie's American Dream*, illustrate the wisdom of mothers who never let their humble circumstances prevent them from raising successful children. Quite the opposite. It made her more determined that they'd have a better life than she did. Maggie Comer's "mother wit" even extended to her choice of toys for her children.

As Mrs. Comer told her son, "We were education-minded in your toys but also we wanted you to have fun. When we could we bought you toys with the alphabetics on them. We bought you a little chair that had the alphabetics written on the back. The table with it had alphabetics and the numbers. When you started to school, all of you, you knew your numbers up to 100 and the alphabetics. And the things that they taught in kindergarten, you helped the teacher teach it because you had gone through that at home.

"Your favorite toy was your doctor's kit," she reminded Dr. Comer. "When you were no more than two and Norman [his brother] was the baby, he was ill and we had called the doctor to come in. The lady that was working for us said to you, 'Don't do that, if you do I'm going to tell the doctor on you when he comes.' And you said, 'I not afraid of doctors. When I get to be a big man I going to be a doctor.'

"Of course, I took you up on that," Maggie Comer goes on to

tell her son. "And after that we started buying a little doctor kit with all those little medicines, which was candy—that made two reasons why you liked to play with the kit, to act like a doctor and to eat candy. If any of us got a little scratch or anything of the kind, we'd say, 'Come on, doc, and wrap my finger.' Some people would say, 'Oh, you know he's never going to be a doctor. Why would you say that?' But we didn't pay attention to them. We just did things our own way. We kept talking up that doctor business, and naturally that's what you went for."

Maggie Comer also understood how important it was to engage children's minds in the early going. "I believe in talking with children, taking time with them, taking them to places of interest, doing things together. But everybody don't see it that way," she recalled. "Some people wish the children off, and they don't bring the children in on any of the things going on in the home. So if they don't bring the children in when they are children at home, how are they going to know when they go out?

"That's what bothers me about so many of our people, they don't talk to their kids. Of course, it's true of a lot of whites, too, but they've got the head [the lead] so I worry about ours. Parents get on a bus and flop down and just sit and stare. But when kids are small, you can teach them a lot. You can read these different advertisements on the ceiling and point out different things. You can say, 'Now that is where Mazola Oil Company's plant is; that's Inland Steel; this is the fire department right here; what do they do at the fire department?' or what have you. Just be talking, answering questions, making them think about things. That's what's wrong with so many children today. Parents only talk to themselves and never discuss things with the children," she says regrettably. "Children see this thing and that thing and don't understand it. They ask Mom or Dad, 'Why is this thing over here?' or 'Why is this man standing here?' You explain to the child and they want to learn more. But you find children that's not talked to—they're very dull."

Maggie Comer knew in her heart what we all know, that every child is born ready and willing to learn. But the sad fact is that as they grow up and move through elementary school, many young-sters lose their natural curiosity and enthusiasm for learning. In its report, the Carnegie Task Force warned that this pattern of under-achievement is especially noticeable for children of low-income families and for minority children. Typically they don't receive the kind of support at home or the type of instruction in school that keeps them turned on to learning. That's why elementary school is a defining experience for children.

It's easy to take the importance of school success for granted. After all, who could disagree that getting good grades is a good thing? But doing well in school has an even deeper importance than many of us realize. As the Carnegie Report reminds us, a child's fundamental sense of worth as a person depends heavily on whether he or she achieves in school. When adults have low expectations for young people and don't support their efforts to achieve, then de-featism sets in. The children don't try to do well, so they don't do well, and it becomes what's called a self-fulfilling prophecy. The children lose interest in learning and perform poorly in school. That hurts their chances to earn a good living and enjoy the fruits of the American Dream.

## WHAT MORE YOU CAN DO

I once attended a breakfast meeting that saluted the excellent work of an educational group that operates wonderful after-school programs. The mother of one participant was called upon to speak. Mind you, she was bright, articulate, and dressed like she was headed right after breakfast to a management job at some corpora-tion. Not surprisingly, she praised the program to the skies. She gushed on and on about how much the program had done for her son, such as offering tutorial assistance after school, taking him on college visits, and alerting him when it was time to send in the fee to take the SAT exam.

I was mighty impressed by the quality of the program. But the more I thought about what she said, the more dismayed I became. Why? Because this obviously "together" parent was basically shirking her fundamental responsibility toward her son and was content to let the program pick up the slack. That's wrong of her and it won't do. Suppose the program was weak? What if the staff dropped a stitch about the SAT deadline? Would the mother ever have noticed? What would have become of her son if she didn't?

"Wise and alert parents do not relinquish responsibility for their children's education," advises author Emma W. Talbott. "They recognize early on that it is a shared responsibility to see that their children receive a good education and develop a worthwhile value system. This is a joint challenge given to family, school, religious institutions, and community."

Home is the core of human life. Or at least it should be for children until they are mature enough to set forth on their own. The responsibilities parents must shoulder and the things they must do to ensure that their children succeed academically may seem daunting at times. There isn't a simple recipe for creating the right home environment. I'm tempted to say you should mix hand-me-down knowledge and on-the-job experience with common sense and a heavy dose of love. That probably isn't far off the mark, but fortunately there's more reliable guidance for parents to go on than that.

After extensive interviews with parents of high-achieving black students, the authors of *Beating the Odds* identified six key parenting skills that are instrumental in raising academically successful children. They are:

1. Demonstrating love through active involvement in your youngster's education, providing support and encouragement, and fostering a belief in self.
2. Setting suitable limits on behavior and imposing discipline when appropriate.
3. Establishing high expectations for academic and other success.

4. Developing open and strong communication with your children.
5. Encouraging children to develop a positive view of their gender and ethnicity.
6. Taking full advantage of available community resources that supplement what parents can do themselves.

Interestingly enough, the mothers who were interviewed for the same study offered some additional advice about how to raise children who do well in school. The tips they mentioned most frequently were:

- Prepare your children for school by providing academic challenges at home.
- Make certain your children are placed in the proper classes, and pressure the school to change the assignment if they are placed in classes below their ability.
- Encourage your children to read.
- Talk to your children's teachers if problems arise at school.
- Encourage your children to become involved in extracurricular activities.
- Take your youngsters on field trips and to work.
- Switch your children to a different school if they aren't getting a solid education where they're currently enrolled.
- Seek help from your extended family network because that's an important source of support and reinforcement.

And what about the fathers of these high-performing students? The authors report that they were more likely to get involved by intervening at school on behalf of their children. They also were more active in discipline-related matters, such as monitoring whether homework was completed and setting limits on their children's overall conduct.

"Parents are an incredible resource for their children, and they should appreciate the tremendous influence they have on their kids," says Karla Ballard of the National Urban League Young Professionals. "Self-esteem is so critical for young people, and when parents act as advocate for their children's educational interests, it really makes a difference. There are people out there who view black children as a drain on society. Parents must reverse this misperception—which is sometimes internalized by the kids themselves—by appreciating both who their children are and who they are striving to be.

"A parent often asks: 'Who am I to be a teacher? I don't have a college degree. I can't understand math, etc.' Yet the value of your life is what's critical. Parents must see themselves as educators and their own lives as educational experiences. Show your children how you make the household budget and pay the bills. Share the history of the family with them. I firmly believe that all experiences—whether good or bad—are jewels and pearls. Parents can take their own personal stories and transform them into individualized educational textbooks for their children."

Ms. Ballard also believes that parents should change the way they see their children. "Put on new glasses when you look at them," she advises. "Just don't judge them with their teachers' eyes. Create a new value system for your kids so you can become an effective advocate for them. I know this from my own personal experience and those of my friends who have succeeded academically despite the odds: if you raise the bar of expectation for your children, they will respond."

The Standard Keepers Program of the New York Urban League conducts workshops that offer parents specific suggestions for how to become effectively involved in their children's education. This ranges from helping with homework to preparing for after-school conferences with teachers, guidance counselors, and principals. The program has found that when children and parents take the time to interact and communicate openly with each other—whether that involves assembling a model plane with your 6-year-old son or sharing stories with your seventh-grade daughter about your own teen years—that promotes bonding between them and actually can boost the child's scholastic performance.

Standard Keepers also conducts an assessment of student needs. The children answer questions about how they feel about their school and home lives. That feedback helps parents learn what might be bothering their children and how they are coping with their frustrations and anxieties. For example, children are asked to circle a face—whether it's smiling, frowning, or expressionless—that best suits how the youngster would answer the following questions:

1. I like going to school.
2. I am happy with my work.
3. I like my teacher.
4. I have many friends.
5. I like doing my homework.
6. I am happy in my family.
7. I like to look at books.
8. I like showing my family my schoolwork.
9. My friends like me.
10. I am happy when I go home from school.

Why not try that exercise with your children and see what you turn up? I expect that what you find out will be revealing and useful in supporting your child's development.

Children in Standard Keepers are also asked to fill out a monthly Parent Report Card. That idea probably makes you really nervous. Yes, they actually grade their parents either A, B, C, D, E, or F in the following areas:

1. Helps me with my homework when I ask.
2. Understands my moods.
3. Gives me hugs.
4. Tells me he or she loves me.
5. Lets me act my age.
6. Is nice to my friends.
7. Keeps my secrets.
8. Helps me look my best.

9. Cooks good meals.
10. Keeps the house nice.
11. Watches TV with me.
12. Listens to my problems.
13. Tries to explain things to me.
14. Doesn't scream at me when they're angry.
15. Thinks about me enough.
16. Spends time with me alone.
17. Makes me laugh.
18. Makes the holidays special.
19. Lets me make my own decisions.
20. Helps me make my room a special place.
21. Helps me get up when I oversleep.
22. Treats all the kids in the family fairly.
23. Answers my questions about sex.
24. Helps me buy things I want.
25. Is understanding when I earn poor grades.

This Standard Keepers questionnaire is pretty deep when you think about it. But the more I reflect on the kind of information that's collected, the more convinced I am that it's incredibly valuable for parents to understand the breadth and depth of their children's feelings. If it's taken to heart, this information can make for smarter and more compassionate parents, and thus for more self-confident and successful kids.

Young people are human beings with basic needs—love, nurturing, support, and direction. There are plenty of perfectly sensible things that parents and caregivers who are really tuned in to these needs can do to cultivate an early thirst for learning and a healthy appetite for school. Believe me, you don't need a college degree to guide your child toward academic success.

"I take care of my five grandchildren who are from five to thirteen years old," says Danny Brown, whose oldest grandson Corey attends the Higher Aims After School Program sponsored by the Westchester Clubmen in White Plains, New York. "I try to teach my boys and girls responsibility and manners because I believe this has a direct effect on how they do in school. I also help them with their homework so they can keep their marks up and not fall behind.

"I've learned how important it is to be patient. You should keep encouraging your children by telling them to do the best they can. You have to help them stay focused because, unfortunately, they're going to encounter a great deal of peer pressure not to study or concentrate on their schooling. I know it might be difficult sometimes, but I'm of the firm belief that when parents and caregivers take an active role in a child's education, it makes a real difference."

## THE EDUCATIONAL HOME FRONT

Earlier I warned that television shouldn't become an electronic baby-sitter or, worst still, a substitute parent. The NAEP report reveals that students who watched three hours or less per day scored higher on the national reading test than children who watched more than three hours of TV daily. What's even more disturbing, black and Hispanic children who are bringing up the rear when it comes to reading performance watch lots more television—an average of three to four hours *each day*—than white children, who read much better and average just two hours and twenty-two minutes a day in front of the TV.

I don't much care whether it's Mom, Dad, or Grandma—someone in authority at home must step in and put their foot down. "Of course I want to be watching TV, but my mother makes me do my homework first," says Lewis, a fifth-grader in an overcrowded public school in Newark. "I think about school all the time when I leave, but not in a good way. I feel a lot of pressure and anxiety about doing my homework. At night, I take out my review sheet from my teacher and my aunt helps me by quizzing me on the questions. I like to study with her because she's smart and organized and lets me go at my own pace. Even though I miss some of the TV programs that my friends talk about, I feel accomplished and smart when I hand in my homework to my teacher."

What else can you do at home to help position your child for academic success? Let me cite some more lessons from *Beating the Odds* that I haven't mentioned yet:

1. Discuss what you and your child see around you.
2. Name objects when children point to them.
3. Look up what you see together in books, dictionaries, encyclopedias, and on the Internet to draw connections.
4. Make workbooks available as soon as your child can hold a crayon.
5. Focus early on math and science.
6. Prepare your children for school with simple math problems and science experiments.
7. Send them to educational summer programs if available.
8. Encourage children to ask questions of people they meet, such as "What kind of work do you do?"
9. Use educational computer and video games that will strengthen learning.
10. Talk to your children on an adult level since this helps them learn more and learn faster.
11. Answer their "why is it that . . ." questions with complete answers.
12. Return to the same places at different points in their lives because they can learn new things from each visit.
13. When necessary, provide tutors if you can afford it, or find a tutorial program if you cannot.
14. Enroll your children in after-school activities such as art classes, dance and music lessons, team sports, church activities, and computer camps, where they get to strengthen their academic skills in a nonacademic setting and practice working with other youngsters in teams.
15. Buy games and equipment that bolster their academic skills, such as Lego, chemistry sets, electric toys, personal comput-

ers for young people, puzzles, building blocks, dinosaur toys, art supplies, Rubik's Cubes, and chess and checker sets.

The problems our young people face in this day and age are very real and often frightening: terrorist attacks, gun violence, drugs, AIDS, racism, and so forth. Your children are old enough to handle the information; don't be hesitant to talk with them about issues that bother them in an open and honest manner. That's vital to their learning and development as well-educated and thoughtful young people.

The learning process entails more than reading and intellectual development per se. Parents must also attend to their children's emotional growth and health. The two are intertwined. Let them know that if there's ever something wrong, they can always come to you to talk about it and together you'll try to figure out a solution.

Beverly Gross-Spencer is the mother of an 8-year-old daughter. She lives in Philadelphia but commutes daily to New York City to work at the National Urban League. Over the years, she has developed the tradition of regularly taking a walk around the block with her daughter when she gets home from work, no matter how tired she might be.

"Usually we only circle the block once and there isn't all that much we need to talk about," Ms. Gross-Spencer explains. "But some days when I arrive, my daughter will say she wants to take that walk. That's a signal there's something on her mind and she needs to unburden herself. It may be what's happening at school. Or it could be tensions with friends. When she tells me we need to take that walk, I drop everything else, and no matter how exhausted I am, we head out. I know that's her code for 'I really need to talk to you, Mommy.' On those occasions, we often go around the block more than once. Even if the weather is bad, we just pull on our boots and face the rain and snow together.

"You really should take the time when your children reach out to you. And you should always be reaching out to them. You may learn something that can defuse a situation or it gives you an opening or opportunity to talk in a way that you can't in another kind of setting. My best friend uses bedtime to have talks with her children."

"My advice to younger kids is to make sure that someone cares about you and don't be afraid to ask for help," says Sonya, a ninth-grader from Kansas City. "Sometimes it can even be an older cousin or neighbor. If you walk around alone with your problems, it can feel scary and interfere with your homework."

Family members and mentors often are important players in a young person's life. Daryl Smith, 35, is a real estate specialist and a member of the San Diego Urban League Young Professionals. "I believe very strongly in giving back to the community," he says. "The African-American population of San Diego is less than 2 percent, and young black professionals have to serve as role models for kids in school. We can help young people learn how to believe in themselves and guide them in following through with their goals or dreams. We can also show them how if one route doesn't work, they can always go another way. We emphasize to our younger brothers and sisters that we would not have succeeded professionally if we had dropped the ball and not completed our education.

"I credit my parents as the key to my academic success. They always took a real interest in my work and what was going on in my life. My father was in the Navy and my mother was a homemaker. Both always stressed the importance of education and took a major role in my schooling. They went to parent-teacher meetings all the time and were in constant contact with my school. They were also very involved in community activities.

"Mentoring is a mutually beneficial relationship because while we're helping these young people stay in school and remain true to themselves, they're helping us stay current and keep on the cutting edge. Our relationship is also a reminder that, in a sense, we are all part of the same family and should be there for each other."

## ACHIEVEMENT BENCHMARKS

Children need to know that you believe education is hugely important and that you want them to do well in school. High expectations set the stage for academic success. But as I was taught in law school, that's necessary but not sufficient. Or as President Ronald Reagan put it even more bluntly in negotiating nuclear missile treaties with the former Soviet Union: "Trust, but verify."

In other words, when it comes to education, high expectations should be coupled with heavy-duty vigilance. Parents should monitor closely whether their kids are mastering the necessary skills and meeting the standards at each age level for what they must know and be able to do. Report cards and feedback from teachers give you some feel for how they're doing. But don't be content with that information. Many school districts have prepared specific academic benchmarks grade by grade which you can use to double-check on your child's progress and quiz the teachers if your child appears to be falling behind.

To cite just one example of these benchmarks, the Board of Education of the City of New York publishes pamphlets for parents that outline the scholastic guidelines pupils should meet from kindergarten through eighth grade. The guidelines cover language arts, math, science, and social studies. Here's a sample of what the school system expects pupils to know and be able to do grade by grade:

### Kindergarten

- Begin choosing books to read, reread, and have read to them.
- Learn new words each day.
- Recognize their own first name.
- Use letters, scribbles, and gestures to tell a story.
- Hear and follow directions.
- Listen respectfully and learn to take turns speaking.
- Use real money to learn the names of coins and bills.

## First Grade

- Read a range of materials including poems, picture books, letters, and simple informational books.
- Recognize and know the sounds of all the letters in the alphabet.
- Write using a combination of correctly spelled words and others with made-up spellings.
- Learn how to make change for amounts of money.
- Begin to acquire information from observation, experimentation, print, and other sources.
- Generate ideas and questions that show inventiveness and originality.

## Second Grade

- Read one or two chapters from a book daily.
- Use their knowledge of all sounds and letters in the alphabet to figure out the meaning of unfamiliar words.
- Have an opportunity to share finished work with an audience.
- Use shapes to create designs.
- Use technology and tools such as magnifiers, scales, thermometers, and computers.
- Explore maps, globes, and atlases, noting symbols, directions, and methods for measuring distance.

## Third Grade

- Be able to write about, discuss, and summarize the plot, setting, character, and main ideas in books they read.
- Keep a collection of their writing.
- Spell most words correctly and notice when a word doesn't look right.
- Add and subtract whole numbers with and without using a calculator.

- Use information gathered from experiments and other sources to explain observations and events.
- Collect and organize information from various sources.

## Fourth Grade

- Read familiar books aloud with accuracy and expression.
- Demonstrate correct use of grammar, including nouns, verbs, and adjectives.
- Use single decimal numbers and percents.
- Develop and describe, both orally and in writing, the behaviors that contribute to good personal health.
- Understand that others might have a different point of view.

## Fifth Grade

- Put together ideas and information from different books, making decisions about what is most important.
- Organize what they will say using notes or other memory tools.
- Demonstrate correct use of punctuation, including quotation marks, commas, and colons.
- Solve everyday problems where fractions are used.
- Ask appropriate questions and use evidence and concepts learned from observations and reliable sources, as well as common sense, to construct explanations for the results of experiments.
- Express opinions and back them up with reasons.

## Sixth Grade

- Use computer software to expand reading choices.
- Learn word processing skills.
- Use calculators for problem solving.
- Use computers to create tables, graphs, and charts.
- Describe a scientific concept and explain a scientific procedure.

## Seventh Grade

- Evaluate how effectively and accurately an author communicates information, opinions, and ideas.
- Write a story that's either fictional or autobiographical.
- Revise work using dictionaries, reference books, and other materials to assist in editing.
- Talk about mathematics and why it's useful in their lives now and in the future.
- Use a variety of methods such as data tables, graphs, and databases to record information.
- Identify current political and social problems and conduct research to understand them and find answers.

## Eighth Grade

- Use online and electronic databases on computers.
- Keep a record of what they've read during the year, including reading goals and accomplishments.
- Use the mathematical ideas and terms accurately.
- Propose and critique alternate explanations for observations and distinguish between fact and fiction.
- Do research with others to come up with group decisions and ideas.
- Acquire information from observation, experimentation, print, and other sources.
- Make connections between information from different texts.

I hope you noticed in looking over the list that plenty of these skills required by the New York City School System can be honed and practiced at home. Like a sturdy foundation that rises higher and higher, these academic skills are built layer by layer year after year. For a detailed list of the school district's standards by grade level, go to the Internet and log on to www.nycenet.edu/DIS/whatdidyou/.

High school isn't the end of the academic line, of course. While you are monitoring your youngsters' progress, it's never too early to start thinking about what lies beyond. Are they likely to go on to college after they graduate? Will it be a two-year community college or a four-year university? Or will they head right for the job market or military service? The route they take is usually guided by the game plan you map out together early on. Remember that 85 percent of the jobs today are skilled and professional positions. The more highly educated your youngsters are, the higher they're likely to rise economically. So college should definitely be in the cards if they can handle the work and you can handle the tuition bills.

Getting your children smack on the achievement page right from the start and making certain they're enrolled in challenging courses all the way through school will put them squarely on the path to college. Monitoring how they do in school will help keep them on course. Consult with your child's school guidance counselor as early as seventh grade to determine the classes your child must take to prepare for college. Students headed for higher education start practicing how to take college entrance exams like the SAT and ACT as early as middle school. So in eighth and ninth grades, you should arrange for your child to take the PSAT (Preliminary Scholastic Assessment Test) in preparation for the SAT (Scholastic Assessment Test).

I must say that making thirteen- and fourteen-year-olds take exams like these strikes me as excessive. But that's the way the college admissions game is played these days. So you and your child have no choice but to understand the rules and then play hard to win by doing well in school and on those entrance exams. By junior year in high school, practice time is over and the game starts being played for keeps. Colleges and universities start checking those test scores and school grades to help them decide which applicants can handle college work and whom they want to admit.

The other game plan parents need to map out in the early going is how they plan on paying those tuition bills. The cost of private universities keeps soaring out of sight, and public universities aren't a piece of cake financially for working families any longer. So high school is the time to start hunting down information on scholar-ships and student loan programs. Many states offer financial assis-tance to achievers who attend state universities.

For many families, their incomes are too low to ask them to sac-rifice any more or save much of anything toward college costs. But most families can make a dent in the financial burden by salting away some money starting as early as elementary school. And also by scaling back their lifestyles along the way, especially at the height of the tuition load when their kids actually are in college.

Neither my wife nor I are clotheshorses, so it was easy for us to wear things until they wore out instead of when they became un-fashionable. When we drove our eldest daughter to college for her freshman year, I told everyone in the family that I hoped they liked our station wagon because I intended to fetch our youngest daugh-ter with it when she graduated from college a decade later. Our car just made it to the finish line. And so did we, by using our savings, stretching out bill payments, and frequently tapping the cash re-serve on our checking account. College is a long-term investment in your child's future that is well worth the short-term sacrifice.

Applying to college, picking which one to attend, and figuring out how to pay for it could fill up another book entirely. Ask your child's guidance counselor for assistance. After all, that's their job. But don't forget the story I told earlier about how my high school counselor gave me a bum steer. That still happens occasionally. As a backup, there are quite a few reputable guidebooks and websites that should prove helpful. (A list is included in the Resource Directory at the end of the book, beginning on page 231.)

Parents chart the course for their children. The same is true of caregivers who have primary responsibility for rearing young peo-ple. "Parents should show you that what you do as a young person will affect you later down the line," says Shawn Barney, 26, who joined the National Urban League's Board of Trustees straight out of college and whose father was a longtime local Urban League CEO. "Since I can remember, my mother and father held me ac-countable for my actions and for pulling my weight. I was supposed to stay out of trouble and do well academically. I knew my parents would be disappointed or angry if I didn't achieve to my fullest capabilities—I always felt I was 'on the hook,' not off it."

Today more than ever before in American history, education is indispensable to economic self-sufficiency and twenty-first-century citizenship. So we are all "on the hook" because high achievement begins at home.

# CHAPTER FIVE

# Navigating the School System

When I was a kid, schools didn't even pretend to educate all children well. In my elementary school, for example, the teachers focused mostly on pupils whom everyone expected to do well. But they made only a halfhearted attempt to educate the rest of the class to high standards. In those days, school districts never published reading scores or dropout rates. It was unheard of back then for school districts or the state commissioner of education to issue highly publicized report cards on individual schools that revealed how their pupils were doing. Nor was there much public pressure to hold schools accountable for their performance.

To tell the truth, teachers concentrated on students like me, who paid attention in class, faithfully did our homework assignments, completed book reports on time, and performed well on tests. So long as they behaved, the other kids were welcome to remain in school until they turned sixteen. Then they could drop out if they wished. If they misbehaved badly, they could be shipped off to reform school in a flash.

Public schools could get away with favoring the few over the many because that suited the way the American economy worked generations ago. The thinking back then was that the economy needed only a handful of highly educated managers and executives. Most young people were destined to become factory workers, farmers, and soldiers. Instead of extensive "book learning," employers looked for workers with strong backs who were industrious and willing to sweat. In exchange, working people, especially those who belonged to labor unions, pretty much could count on earning a solid living that enabled them to buy a home and a car, take an occasional vacation, and send their children to college.

That's ancient history now. Public schools have come under intense criticism and pressure in recent years, for good reason. In this day and age, we expect schools to educate all children well. Fairness demands it, and the labor market, dominated by all those skilled and professional jobs, requires it.

Parents, employers, and politicians have become impatient with the fact that millions of American youngsters are so poorly educated and unprepared for the job market. I don't blame them! This *Preparation Gap* is widest for children who are African American, Latino, and Native American, or from low-income urban and rural communities. Closing the gap is key to getting these youngsters into the economic mainstream.

Parents and caregivers owe it to the children they're raising to take an active role in ensuring that their youngsters receive the best education available to equip them for success. That means being informed enough plus determined enough to ask point-blank questions, get answers, and make smart decisions about the kind of education that is best for your child. The worst thing imaginable is to be missing in action. Not only will your children get the impression that their education isn't important to you, but their schools will also be lulled into believing they can shortchange your child without being caught or worrying about the consequences. For the sake of your child, you must not allow educators to get away with that kind of thinking.

## KNOWLEDGE IS POWER

"There was an *assumption* on the part of the principal that my physically active six-year-old son belonged in special education, even though he was one of the brightest kids in his class," says James, a lawyer from Washington, D.C. "Believe me, it was more intimidating facing a committee of 'experts' trying to convince me to put my boy in special ed classes than arguing a case in front of a hostile jury. I can only imagine what other parents must also go through."

I realize we're all busy, putting in those extra hours on the job. I know how wiped out most of us are when we get home after work. As they say, "Been there, done that." My wife and I faced the same demands from our jobs and drains on our time when our children were going through school. Like millions of other folks who work in New York City, we both endured a one-hour commute at the beginning and end of the workday.

But no matter how busy we are, parents don't have time in this day and age not to have time to get deeply involved in our children's education. To get schooled, so to speak, on how schools work; what they teach; how they judge their students; whether teachers are qualified; when assignment to special ed is all right vs. all wrong for your child; how students are selected for honors courses and gifted programs; how to steer your own children into challenging courses; and what to do if they slip behind. By learning how to monitor and navigate the school system, you are letting both your youngsters and their teachers know that how they're doing in school matters enormously to you and that you're keeping an eagle eye on the situation.

Parents who feel uncomfortable playing this role because they don't believe they know enough can turn to someone they trust to help out and to intercede. Solicit the help of relatives or friends. Ask your pastor or deaconess in church for advice and help. Seek out a community agency such as the local Urban League, Boys or Girls Club, or YMCA. Above all, try not to let yourself feel intimidated by a lot of bureaucracy and official jargon. Figuring out the nuts and bolts of how schooling works isn't as perplexing as it may appear at first.

Public schools often fall short of educating children to their fullest potential. That's especially true of schools in low-income urban and rural communities. Only a handful of minority youngsters ever get to take honors courses. They are steered instead to less challenging courses and special education. The result is that minority children usually aren't challenged academically, so it's little wonder they don't test well or score as highly on standardized exams.

Far too few inner-city high schools offer academically tough Advanced Placement (AP) courses. Even when they do, those classes may not be nearly as rigorous as they should be. A summer intern at the National Urban League named Travis Bristol once dropped by my office to introduce himself. He'd just finished his freshman year at Amherst College, my alma mater. When I asked how it had gone, he said the first year had been rough. One reason was the writing assignments he was expected to complete every week. I asked why that had been such a struggle. Travis replied that he'd written only one 4½-page paper during his entire high school career. This even though he'd actually taken two AP courses at his New York City high school. When I quizzed him on what kind of writing he'd done in those courses that were reputed to be so rough, he said the teachers only had them write 300-word essays so they could "get over" on the AP test.

Many of us bitterly recall being underestimated or misled by supposedly well-meaning teachers and guidance counselors who, it turned out, had anything but our best interests at heart. I already told you how my self-confidence was badly shaken when I was informed that I should not count on getting into graduate or professional school even though I had earned excellent grades in high school. Many African-American parents report similar experiences with school systems they consider to be unsupportive, culturally insensitive, or even outright discriminatory. Unfortunately, there are countless examples of this type of "institutional racism," a subtle and malicious, behind-the-scenes way that minority children can be held back or routed down the wrong path.

When I was coming along, public schools seemed to subscribe to the philosophy of survival of the fittest. In many respects they still do, even though society today expects much, much more—as it should. We expect schools to educate all youngsters well, and we have every right to expect them to as a matter of equity, equality, and global economic competitiveness.

Yet public education still hasn't restructured the way it operates to accommodate this new mission. The fact that this is the case was driven home to me when we registered our eldest daughter for the ninth grade after our family moved to New Rochelle. She'd done very well academically in New Haven, where we used to live. In fact, when she was an eighth-grader, we rustled up the money to send her to an excellent private day school because the public middle school there was so weak.

Our daughter's new school placed her a notch below "honors," which angered us because her previous academic record clearly justified placing her in the swiftest academic pathway available. We accepted tracking in those days and sought the maximum advantage for our children. We weren't tuned in at the time to the failings of tracking or the fact that youngsters with less impressive academic credentials could profit from taking challenging courses without undercutting the education of strong students. Few parents of high achievers probably believe that, but the evidence on the benefits for everyone of ending tracking is pretty clear.

Anyway, my wife tried to intervene and correct the inappropriate placement. However, the teachers refused to bend. Determined to reverse the situation before too much of the school year elapsed, I decided to visit the school. After all, I had plenty of time on my hands because I was working for *The New York Times* and it was shut down because of a citywide newspaper strike.

Now you need to understand that when black fathers visit school, that's a very big deal. The teachers are so surprised and unnerved they don't know whether to rejoice by calling the press, or worry and summon the police. I'm just kidding, of course, but it isn't far from the truth. I got dressed that early September morning and went downstairs to the closet, where I pulled my "attitude" off the hanger and put it on. Then I headed over to my daughter's school.

When I asked the teacher why she'd placed our daughter in a track beneath her proven ability, I was given two answers, both of which astonished and appalled me. First, the teacher said, we should be satisfied with where she'd been placed because she would be very well served where they had assigned her. I responded politely that while I suspected she would be well served, she didn't belong there because she unquestionably was an honors student. That's where she belonged, I insisted.

The teacher's second explanation flabbergasted me even more. It revealed what the real deal was. She told me that the honors classes were filled up and that there was a long waiting list of youngsters born in New Rochelle who'd gone through the local schools. Their parents wanted them placed in honors. It was unrealistic to think that a newcomer like our daughter could jump the line ahead of youngsters already in the school system. I allowed as how I understood her point, but I didn't care. Our daughter belonged in honors and we wanted her placed there.

When you think about it, that second reason speaks volumes about what's wrong with schools today. The school system had a long list of youngsters, of all races, who wanted the most challenging courses the schools could offer. Yet they were hoarding honors slots for a handful of youngsters.

That kind of elitist thinking is woefully outmoded today. Why not offer the best to every student who wants it? If that means two-thirds of the student body takes honors, so be it. That's great for them, for the country, and for the U.S. economy because they'll be that much more prepared and productive. The knowledge economy of the twenty-first century requires that America's schools educate all children to their fullest potential. Holding any youngster back holds our economy back. It's downright unfair to children who are shortchanged and it's just plain dumb from society's perspective.

When I couldn't get any satisfaction from my daughter's teacher, I refused to accept her verdict. So I told her politely but firmly that I intended to call the school superintendent first thing the following morning to straighten this out. The next day, before I could even place that call, the school phoned to say our daughter had been elevated to honors effective that day. Clearly, our decision to intervene and our willingness to appeal a ruling we didn't like all the way to the top made a difference in the caliber of education our daughter ended up receiving.

This incident illustrates how parents have to fight for the best interests of their children. Too often parents defer to the teachers and principals as experts about what's best for their child. While the idea isn't to go to war with the school at every turn, parents have to stand up for their children and insist that the school educate them well and up to their fullest potential. Let me also say that it's critically important for both parents to get involved if humanly possible, even if they aren't together. When it comes to educating your children, this shouldn't be seen exclusively as woman's work. That's because it isn't. Remember the impact that my visit to my daughter's school had. They tried rejecting my wife's plea, but we didn't let them get away with rejecting both of us.

Children, and especially boys, need to know that education is critically important to fathers. That their fathers care and are on the case. This isn't about gender superiority. It's about surrounding your children with love and support. It's about sending the signal that "Achievement Matters" in every direction from every direction, so there's no escaping it or ignoring it.

I look to my own father as my inspiration and guide. As I mentioned earlier, in spite of his grueling medical practice, my father was at every important event involving my brother or me at any school we attended. It might be a play or high school cadet parade we were in, an awards assembly, or of course, a graduation ceremony. And he didn't come to these events grudgingly, like it was some kind of obligation. He really was into it, the way a parent should be.

We knew that education really mattered to Mom and Dad. While they didn't do our homework for us, we always knew they were there, that they were monitoring how we were doing from one report card to the next, that the school knew they were watchful, and that they wouldn't hesitate to intervene if we drifted off course.

Nor did they retire as involved parents when I graduated from high school. In college, the social life got really good to me. After all those years of being dutiful about school, at the beginning of my junior year I moved into a fraternity house and started sloughing off scholastically. I had a car and a girlfriend to go along with fraternity life. The car was a VW "Beetle" that I'd bought with my own money saved up from summer jobs.

My grades that first marking period plunged faster than stocks in a bear market. In those days, colleges sent your grades home to your parents, on the perfectly sensible theory that since they were paying the bills, they were entitled to check the return on their investment. Somewhere along the way, college students became "emancipated." So even though parents still foot the bills, colleges keep them in the dark about their kid's grades. Only the undergraduates know, and parents must get the grades from them. Makes no sense whatsoever to me, but that's the way it is.

Anyway, Dad spotted those dreadful grades and, as was his style, wrote me a very calm letter I'll never forget. He said there was a two-car garage behind the house and one of the spaces was vacant. The unspoken message was that if my grades didn't improve by next marketing period, my "Beetle" would be parked in that garage, no matter whose name was on the title certificate. I heard him and heeded his message without any hesitation or backtalk. That's because by being there for me all along, he'd shown me that all he wanted was the best for me.

I've never forgotten how committed my parents were to my education. Knowing they were there gave me direction and strength. It gave me courage and encouragement. Above all, it gave me a frame of reference and set of expectations. They were on my case and on the school's case if need be. And that's where each of us must be if we're to bring that familiar saying, "All children can learn" alive for every child.

## JUDGING THE EFFECTIVENESS OF SCHOOLS

How can parents evaluate and judge the academic standards of their children's schools? The Education Trust, a highly respected research and advocacy organization in Washington, D.C., released an instructive survey in 1999 of several hundred high-performing high schools across the country that serve minority and low-income children. Many of them outshine even suburban schools on state tests. Educators everywhere could learn a lot from these schools. Parents can use these pointers to appraise whether their children's schools work as well as they should. What characteristics do the schools spotlighted by the Education Trust share in common?

- They devote lots more time than the typical school to reading and math instruction, even if that means lengthening the school day.
- They monitor their students closely and intervene quickly if the students falter. They don't dawdle during the school year and then impose massive doses of summer school after the students fall way behind.
- They get parents involved, not just with staging bake sales, but also with helping their children to do better in school and meet the standards.
- They place the burden for improvement mainly on the educators, where it belongs.

Without a doubt, there are urban schools serving minority and low-income pupils that operate this way and get the job done—not just for a few, but for the vast majority of youngsters. The very existence of these schools removes any lingering excuse for the failure of other schools to equip our children to perform at grade level or better in such fundamental subject areas as reading, writing, and math.

States that impose high standards and school systems that implement them share responsibility for:

- Focusing schools first on instilling the fundamental skills and then building on that foundation.
- Investing in qualified teachers and high-quality teaching.
- Ensuring that those who teach our children believe they can achieve.
- Providing effective professional development for teachers and principals.
- Making sure parents are active and respected partners in the educational process.
- Giving principals and teachers the authority to succeed while holding them accountable should they consistently fail to deliver for our youngsters.
- Providing sufficient funding to ensure high-quality education.
- Enacting policies, practices, and labor agreements that place high achievement for children first.

It's up to us as parents and caregivers to understand how our children's schools work—or at least are supposed to work—so we can maneuver our way through the educational maze to get the best results for our children.

## THE NEW HAVEN INITIATIVE

Accountability in education isn't confined to meeting the standards and regulations imposed by various layers of government, from the local district to the state and the feds. In my opinion, true accountability means meeting the educational needs of children and parents who put their faith in a school system and trust it to cultivate the potential of its pupils and equip them academically for adulthood.

The good news is that accountability in education is not a pipe dream that's out of reach. Let me turn again to New Haven, Connecticut, to illustrate this point. Students in the public schools are mostly poor, heavily minority, and chronically underachieving. The district's standardized test scores routinely rank among the worst in the state. School superintendent Reginald Mayo and Dr. James Comer, who started the School Development Program that our daughter enrolled in, have joined forces to create a bold new education initiative that, according to *The New York Times*, "takes the concept of accountability to a level that state officials say is unique in Connecticut and perhaps the nation."

The strategy was designed over the course of two years by a 27-member committee consisting of local parents, business leaders, academics, and social services representatives in the region. The revolutionary change—as compared to business as usual—is that New Haven's accountability plan views student achievement as a shared responsibility of the entire community, instead of strictly the job of the schools.

"In most other strategies for accountability, they look at test scores and then they take punitive actions against teachers and administrators when the scores are deemed too low," explains Dr. Comer. "We're going to make people aware of what is necessary and try and be helpful. We will set the expectation that they will participate." Here are some highlights of how it works:

- Teachers not only instruct students; they also advise and encourage parents who might be having trouble keeping their children in school.
- School administrators call on local businesses for volunteers to counsel students and parents who need extra help, as well as asking the companies for money, computers, and other donations.
- Religious leaders use their houses of worship to announce the names of Honor Roll students and their parents seated in the pews.

"Parents never did not care, they just did not know how to navigate the system," says Sabrina Bruno, former president of the New Haven Parent Teacher Organization. "Parents have often felt that teachers were talking to them in a different language. It made them feel very inferior and intimidated."

The New Haven plan is a positive step in the direction of recognizing how vitally important it is for parents to understand: (1) what these academic standards mean; (2) why it's essential for your child to meet or exceed them; (3) how schools and school systems work; and (4) how to navigate the school bureaucracy to secure the high caliber of education your child requires and deserves. The need to know how to do this starts with day care and nursery school, and continues right through to applying to college.

By making parents and caregivers respected partners in the educational process, they become more at ease and effective in communicating to and collaborating with teachers, guidance counselors, school psychologists, and principals. That way, shared accountability is a win-win situation for everyone involved, starting with the children. Getting the best education possible for your child isn't simply a matter of knowing the right questions to ask. Parents and caregivers must also gain the self-confidence and savvy to insist on answers and solutions that serve their child's best interests.

## EDUCATIONAL BUZZ WORDS

In order to participate effectively and be in a position to appraise your child's school, it's helpful to have a working knowledge of some "hot button" issues you're likely to encounter along the way. I'm talking about educational buzz words and the spirited debates behind them, such as: *standards, assessments, high-stakes tests, accountability, school choice, vouchers, and charter schools.* Here's a quick explanation of each one:

1. *Standards* are what state education agencies and local school districts say students should know and be able to do in order to ad-

vance from one grade to the next and ultimately graduate from high school. There's a set of standards for each core subject grade by grade.

"We educate parents about the standards set by the New York City Board of Education and how their children are expected to perform at their individual grade level," says LaVerne Bloomfield-Jiles of the New York Urban League's Standard Keepers Program. "In this way, parents become the true keepers of the standards for their children and don't have to rely solely on a system that often prepares students with the minimum possible standards it can get away with. Parent ambassadors are then chosen from the program to train other parents and caregivers on a grassroots level in order to reach as many members of the community as possible."

Every school system has certain set standards. Knowing what they are helps ensure that your child will meet them and hopefully even exceed them.

2. *Assessments* refer to the way that classroom teachers, school districts, and states go about measuring how well your child is doing in school. They use various methods to do so. Teachers typically take account of performance on tests, classroom participation, and attendance. They may also use so-called "portfolios," which are collections of a student's work, such as original essays they've written, papers they have researched and prepared, and science projects they've completed. States and school districts generally require that all students take what's called standardized tests. That means every student in a given grade and course takes the same exam so the performance of different schools and kinds of students can be compared.

3. *High-stakes tests* are taken by all students in a certain grade to determine whether they have sufficiently mastered the required course material to move on to the next grade. States typically demand that school districts administer these exams. Students who earn a passing mark can move to the next grade. Those who don't may be held back or forced to attend summer school. School systems are cracking down on "social promotion," which is the practice of promoting pupils to the next grade even though they

performed very poorly in the current one. Ending social promotion has sparked heated debates because some students who are held back repeatedly are more prone to drop out of school eventually.

High-stakes tests are generally administered at the end of the fourth, eighth, and eleventh grades, although this may vary by state. Pupils who don't pass the last of these exams may be forbidden to graduate from high school. Like them or not, these tests are a fact of public school life these days all across the country. A serious problem that has surfaced with these tests is that they aren't always in synch with the state academic standards. What's more, the standards and tests don't always match up with what's taught in the classroom. You should keep track of this issue and get involved if it arises in your school district because a serious mismatch between what's tested, what's expected, and what's taught is unfair to the students.

Parents have a huge stake in making sure their youngsters take school seriously and providing them with the necessary guidance and support at home, so they can pass these high-stakes tests. Failure isn't an option given how essential a high school education is for landing a good job.

4. *Accountability* is the equivalent of high-stakes tests for educators, individual schools, and school districts. If students do poorly year after year, state education agencies or school districts may conclude that the problem lies more with the adults than the children. Makes sense to me. Individual teachers whose students repeatedly perform poorly may be reassigned or removed. If failure is school-wide, the district or the state could place it on a watch list or probation. They're given deadlines to boost student performance. If things still don't improve, the school district could resort to replacing the principal and the whole faculty (this drastic remedy is often called "reconstitution"), converting it to a charter school under new management, or closing the school entirely. States like Florida even go so far as to grant students in chronically failing public schools the right to transfer to another school if theirs doesn't improve significantly within several years.

5. *School choice* is both a lofty principle and a pretty common practice. The principle holds that parents should have the right to send their children to whatever school they want, rather than the one they're assigned to. In some cities, parents can even send their youngsters to private or parochial schools at taxpayer expense. Some patient yet energetic parents even choose to educate their children themselves. That's called home schooling.

In practice, enterprising parents exercise choice in a variety of ways. Those with enough money often move to neighborhoods with good schools. Or, they may enroll their youngsters in alternative schools such as magnet schools, theme schools, career academies, charter schools, or highly selective schools, such as Boston Latin or Bronx High School of Science. Under some state regulatory schemes, parents can opt to send their child to another school if the one he or she attends performs miserably year after year. Generally it's the aggressive parents who look for alternatives if they don't like what they see in their child's current school.

Although I'm not Catholic, it's time for confession. When I was about to enter high school, my folks and I figured out how to game the system. The school I was supposed to attend wasn't the strongest academically. The rule back then in Washington was that if another high school offered some course that wasn't available at the school you were assigned to, you could petition to attend the one you prefered to attend. We decided that I simply *had* to study German since, as a strong math and science student, I expected to take courses in which it was convenient to know some German. The high school we targeted offered German, while the other didn't. Bingo, I enrolled in my school of choice, even though it meant riding a bus halfway across the city every day.

6. *Vouchers* are used by parents to help pay tuition for their children at nonpublic schools. In essence, some of the tax money collected for education ends up at private, parochial, and other religious schools instead of all of it going only to public schools. Vouchers subsidize the ability of parents to exercise school choice. This option, which has been offered in cities such as Milwaukee

and Cleveland, is the subject of heated debates and bitter lawsuits. Boiling the controversy down to the basics, advocates of vouchers contend that the government should provide low-income and working families with financial aid so they can afford the choice of sending their children to nonpublic schools the way prosperous parents do. I count myself among the opponents of vouchers who believe that public money shouldn't be spent for nonpublic schools, that vouchers violate the separation of church and state prescribed by the U.S. Constitution, and that they drain tax dollars from struggling public schools that desperately need more money, not less.

I'll lay my views about vouchers on the line. Vouchers would benefit the few, but harm the many educationally. I understand why parents like vouchers, but I'm convinced they'd undermine public schools if the policy ever became widespread. Let me add in the next breath, though, that public schools that consistently fail our kids had better, as my parents used to say, straighten up and fly right in a hurry, or else more and more parents will demand vouchers so they can send their children to effective schools. The bottom line is parents should have zero tolerance for lousy schools in the twenty-first century.

7. *Charter schools* are public schools that operate by different rules than regular schools do. They tend to be smaller and newer than traditional schools. Usually they are exempt from some bureaucratic regulations and they're given much more leeway than regular schools when it comes to hiring and firing teachers and deciding exactly how their budget will be spent. Most states have enacted laws that authorize the creation of charter schools. As of 2001, the number of charter schools in the nation was approaching 2,000.

The basic idea behind charter schools is that "one size doesn't fit all" in K–12 education. So states and local school districts may be allowed under the law to authorize the creation of charter schools that serve as an option for parents and children who are disenchanted with their current school. Since many charter schools are popular and they aren't required to accept every interested child, selection can be by lottery and there could be a lengthy waiting list.

In his book, *The Parent's Complete Guide to Charter Schools,* Frederick A. Birkett, director of the Benjamin Banneker Charter School in Cambridge, Massachusetts, describes the three basic kinds of charter schools as:

1. Created from scratch by parents, teachers, and community members with a particular approach to educating children.
2. Created by the local school district. Operated independently and exempted from certain district regulations, the charter school still remains part of the local public school system.
3. A newly created, independent school run by a for-profit management company, which usually has control over the curriculum used and the hiring of teachers and staff.

Various kinds of organizations can petition to operate charter schools. Universities and cultural institutions are in the business. So are respected community centers, along with some local Urban League affiliates. Typically charter schools are created out of whole cloth, but there are exceptions. Sometimes existing schools that are struggling can be converted to charter schools in order to shake things up and get a fresh start with a new cast of educators and set of rules.

Charter schools are a viable option for minority children. As recently as 1999, blacks constituted nearly one-fourth of the students in these schools. As with any enterprise involving people, success isn't automatic. Some charter schools fall short because they are poorly run, or the well-meaning founders have little clue about what they are doing, or the entity that issues the charter cuts them too much slack and doesn't hold them accountable for their results.

When they are soundly conceived and well run, though, wonderful things can happen for children. Take the New Leadership Charter School, which is a partnership between the Springfield (MA) Urban League and the Massachusetts National Guard. It opened for business in September 1998. When they enrolled, 70 percent of the students scored below grade in reading and math, many of them two grades or more behind. The innovative school focuses on the academic fundamentals. Yet it also emphasizes leadership development and "followership," so young people learn to work for supervisors and serve customers when they grow up without losing their sense of self-respect. It operates 5½ days per week and 230 days out of the year, as opposed to the 180-day calendar for conventional schools. Summer offers special opportunities for outdoor learning, character building, and leadership development, under the tutelage of National Guard mentors.

The students' own testimonials convey the benefits of the experience. As 12-year-old Eduardo Figueroa said, "This school has made me more disciplined and prepared, in all ways. Kids do better here. We're motivated because we see what can get us far in life. We help each other out." Adds Brittany Allen, also age 12: "It's really changed me, this place. Before, I wasn't that focused. Here, you know what you need to do, and you just do it."

The stimulating educational experience has translated already into encouraging academic results. In the fall of 1999, one-third of the pupils began the school year on or above grade in math. Forty-four percent ended the year on grade or better. In reading, 36 percent started out on grade or better. Forty-nine percent finished on or above grade. Charter schools show that in the world of public education where "one size doesn't fit all," there are some shoes that fit certain children very well.

The entire educational landscape in this country is changing rapidly. Parents need to be informed and keep up with the latest developments, requirements, and criteria that will determine both the course and the quality of their children's academic future. Like being a tourist in an unfamiliar country, knowing the language is the first step in understanding the terrain and ultimately mastering the game.

# WHAT TO LOOK FOR IN YOUR CHILD'S SCHOOL

What we think of public schools is changing the more we learn about what's expected of our children. A National Urban League survey in 2001 reflects the mixed views of black Americans toward public schools. One-third of the respondents expressed little confidence in the ability of the schools to educate black children well. The same number of respondents had some confidence. Only one-fourth of them indicated they had a great deal of confidence in public schools.

When judging the quality of your child's school, what factors should you consider? How do you know if the teachers are up to the job? Do you know if the principal is committed to high achievement for all the students? Does the superintendent of schools have sufficient power and community support to impose necessary changes? Does the school board place student achievement at the very top of its totem pole of priorities? Here's what I'd be sure I knew if I were you:

1. *Learn as much as you can about the teachers.* Sometimes you have to take on the school principal and even the school system to make sure your children's teachers know their stuff and genuinely believe that your youngsters can achieve. If they flunk on both counts, they have no business in the classroom, I don't care how neighborly or nice they are.

When our youngest daughter was in high school, she took physics, just like her older sisters. Unbeknownst to us, the previous teacher, whom our middle daughter liked and who'd done such a good job, had moved to a different school. Our daughter really struggled in the early going, but she kept it to herself, thinking she was missing something. She was downright miserable. Yet we weren't as tuned in at the time as we should have been because we'd begun cutting back our involvement now that she was in high school. Big mistake.

We began hearing other parents with kids in the same class complain. So we went over for meet-the-teacher night that fall, where we met her physics teacher. He was a very personable man who undoubtedly paid taxes on his house and college tuition for his own kids. But we discovered from his confusing presentation to the parents that he didn't have a firm handle on the subject matter, much less how to teach it. Alarmed, we joined with other parents in insisting that the principal send in a replacement, which happened.

"Ultimately, it's the parents who are responsible for their children's education and for making sure that the teachers and principal of the school are performing up to par," says Maurice Wilson, director of Employment, Training, and Technology for the San Diego Urban League. "No one can do a better job than a concerned and loving adult who makes it his or her business to stay involved and informed."

Mr. Wilson often finds himself in the role of patching up the frayed lines of communication that can develop between parent and teacher. "I was in the Navy for twenty-six years and remain a firm believer in clear and concise interaction between two parties," he says. "When there's a problem, the situation can get very emotional. The parent will say, 'What's wrong with the way you're teaching my child?' And the teacher will respond, 'What's wrong with your child?' The most important rule for both sides is to keep the focus on what's best for the child, and put your ego to the side."

One of the closely guarded secrets of urban schools is how few of the teachers really are qualified to teach their subjects, especially math and science. Parents should find out whether their children's teachers are certified in the subject they actually teach or at least have majored in it and, along with that, how committed they are to the children in their classroom. Get this information from the principal and seek it for the entire faculty so you'll know whether your child is likely to get qualified teachers all along the way.

This can be tricky because many of us feel at a disadvantage when quizzing teachers about their credentials and the methods and practices they use to educate our children. Keeping this in mind, the Standard Keepers Program prepared a list of relevant questions for parents to refer to when dealing with their children's teachers. Parents are first advised to review their child's report card and test results carefully, then arrange for a face-to-face meeting with the teacher so they can have these items explained in further detail. This publication by Standard Keepers is called "What Parents Can/Should Ask Teachers" and it lists the following kinds of questions:

1. What is your homework policy?
2. What is your grading policy?
3. Is my child's performance based on a comparison to the other children in the class, or is it measured against the school district's academic standards using a scoring card?
4. What is the level of work that meets those "standards"?
5. Can I see sample copies of student work at different levels of mastery?
6. Are tests matched up with the academic standards? How?
7. If my child gets an A+ in your class, will it be viewed as an A+ in another teacher's class in this school or across the school district? In other words, does your grade reflect quality work that would be recognized as A+ anywhere my child goes to school?

If possible, you should be informed of the rights, rules, and policies of your children's schools in writing. This way, you will know how to track your child's progress and what to do if he or she drifts off course. That's real accountability—teachers and parents accountable to one another and both on the hook for the children.

I should warn you that parents and caregivers aren't always welcomed at school with open arms. They're happy to have you attend bake sales. But some teachers and principals are wary of really involved parents because they view it as a bother or none of the parents' business. "Sometimes a teacher can turn against the child when a parent gets involved, but you can't let this stop you," advises Yasmin Enoch, a Brooklyn mother. "Parents must learn to maneuver the system so they don't get frustrated. I almost removed my kids from school and did home schooling until I joined the Standard Keepers Program and learned how to work through the system. You need courage to go to the right people. For example, my older son was asthmatic and they didn't know what to do with him in preschool and kindergarten. I had to keep talking to the people in his school until they understood how to handle his special needs.

"I find that from kindergarten through third grade, kids run home to Mommy and Daddy if there are problems in school. Then, at around nine years of age they begin keeping problems to themselves, especially how they're being treated at school. That's when parents often give over authority to the teacher. 'Why would your teacher lie?' we ask our child. Parents should think back to what they went through when they were young, and listen to both the teacher and your child."

Teachers can make a critical difference in a young person's life, either positively or negatively. We all have examples from our own school years, and most of us can still recite the name of that fifth-grade teacher who told us we could write well or the ninth-grade math teacher who encouraged us to apply for Advanced Placement algebra. To this day, I remember my homeroom teacher in high school, Ms. Anderson, who really believed in me and pushed me to excel. Earlier in the book, I recalled that racist guidance counselor who gave me bad advice. Ms. Anderson, who also was white, backed me every step of the way. Her support definitely inspired me and I didn't want to disappoint her by doing poorly.

Claude, a retired bus driver from Philadelphia, is still bitter about being talked out of pursuing his academic dream by his high school science teacher. "Sixty years ago, I told her that I wanted to be a civil engineer," he explains, "and was told flat out: 'You can't do it.' The system failed me and defined the course I eventually took in life. When my children were in school, I wasn't impressed by their teachers either. You can have numerous degrees, but if you can't impart information to your students, then what are you doing in the classroom?"

Twenty-six-year-old National Urban League trustee Shawn Barney had the exact opposite experience from Claude. "I will never forget my fourth- and sixth-grade public school teacher, Mrs. Peychaud," he says. "She instilled in me and in every student in her class the feeling that we were smart and special. She cared about us inside and outside the classroom and gave us a feeling of esteem. I knew that Mrs. Peychaud would never accept an excuse for my not doing well because I believed in my heart that she cared about me, not only as her student but also as a person."

Parents must keep an open line of communication with their children's teachers. It's absolutely essential to attend parent-teacher nights, schedule parent-teacher conferences, and become active in the school's PTA. Children need to know from adults that their presence in school, the work that they're doing, and the issues they face every day in school are important to the caring adults in their lives. Showing up for these meetings is a way of communicating to your children that you appreciate their efforts. It also lets the teacher know that you're paying attention, so your children are less likely to be overlooked or ignored.

2. *Find out what you're not being told.* What is the school's policy on tracking? Who decides how students qualify for honors classes and gifted programs, and how many are admitted? Why are some children selected for special ed and others not?

Racial profiling in how youngsters are tracked academically remains a huge problem for African-American children. According to the authors of *Beating the Odds: Raising Academically Successful African American Males,* "Black students are more often tracked into lower ability groups involving general education and vocational education and, in contrast, very few black students are placed in gifted classes. As a result of the disproportionate representation in lower-level classes, African-American males receive far less education than their white counterparts. In light of their inadequate education, it is not surprising to see that African-American students earn lower SAT scores and are less well prepared for college."

Teachers refer students for special education classes based on poor academic performance, behavioral difficulties, and oftentimes both. Children who might have a learning disorder, physical handicap, or mental disability can find themselves placed with students who are defined as "acting up" by their teachers. In any case, once children are labeled as a "problem," forced to attend classes apart from other children, and in some districts, required to travel to a different school, they are routed onto a highway to nowhere academically. Their self-esteem suffers. With each passing school year, it's harder and harder to get back on the regular route where the "normal" children are.

Parents often feel pressured to place their children into special ed by school personnel who advise them that this is the most beneficial way—and maybe the only way—for their children to get by. After listening to educators who supposedly know what's best for your child, it's little wonder that so few parents call "time out" and insist on second opinions or other options, such as transfering to a different classroom or school. Special education must be overhauled because schools are using it as a dumping ground for children who may be a challenge to educate but who, in truth, aren't physically or mentally handicapped. Parents should add their voice to this debate by refusing to let their youngsters be assigned to special ed without carefully questioning the reason why.

Tracking often becomes a self-fulfilling prophecy. "My 13-year-old grandson is afraid of being pulled out of special ed," says Yvonne, a home health aide from Greenville, North Carolina. "Most of the kids in the mainstream and honors classes at his school are white, so he'd rather be with his friends in special ed."

Don't let schools and teachers shake your child's confidence and end up afraid and pressured not to succeed like Yvonne's grandson. Figure out your child's interests, style of learning, and ability to achieve. No matter what, don't accept assessments and evaluations at face value if the school tells you something different about a youngster you are rearing, be it your own child, a nephew, a granddaughter, or even someone you are mentoring.

3. *Learn what is expected of your child.* The summer before

school starts is a good time to begin learning what you need to know about your child's school. Check into what percentage of the pupils passed the state exams in key subjects such as reading and math. If the percentage was high—for example, 80 percent or better—then you know that the school pretty much has its act together. Your challenge is to make sure your children learn what they should and end up in the "pass" column on those exams. If the pass rate is much lower, then that's a signal the school may have some bigger problems that bear watching closely.

This is also a good time to check out the qualifications of the faculty. Which teachers are certified in their subjects and which aren't? For those who aren't, there are additional questions you'll want answers to, namely what percentage of that teacher's pupils passed those key exams the previous couple of years. If their pass rate is really low, then I'd urge you to try to prevent your child from being assigned to teachers with a lousy track record.

Come September it's time to arrange to meet your child's teachers and counselors, along with the principal. That initial contact establishes that you're on the case. Have the principal or assistant principal explain the school policies and procedures. There are questions you should ask the teacher so everyone is clear on what's expected of your child in the year ahead. You might begin with: Now what exactly is my child supposed to learn this year? What, specifically, can I do to help make certain my daughter reaches her fullest potential? Will you promise to contact me the instant you spot any signs that my son is slipping backward or falling below grade level in key subjects?

Keep on asking those questions: What will my child be tested on? When will those high-stakes tests be given? What will you do and what can I do to ensure that my son does well on those tests? What'll happen if he doesn't pass? Will he get a second chance? When? Will he be sent to summer school or held back? What kind of instruction will be available if my daughter repeats a grade? What's the success rate for students who are held back?

Parents need to know as much as possible so they can steer their youngsters in the right direction. Education is a lifelong journey of the mind. The destination is academic success, followed in adulthood by personal fulfillment and economic self-sufficiency. Your children depend heavily on you to help them safely navigate the early going. And that's listed just below everlasting love in the job description for parents and caregivers.

# CHAPTER SIX

## Learning Isn't Over When the Last Bell Rings

I first became an expert on the subject of after-school programs back in the fourth grade. That's about the age when my mother started letting me go over to Raymond Playground when school let out. It was where the city's Parks and Recreation Department ran a bunch of art and sports activities in the afternoons and over the summer. This arrangement was rather odd in those days of racial segregation. Remember—Washington, D.C., was basically a Southern town back then. Under the law, black kids like me couldn't attend Raymond Elementary School, which was run by D.C.'s Board of Education. But we could participate in the after-school programs run by the City's Park-Rec Department. Go figure.

When I was growing up, our junior high and high schools stayed open almost until dinnertime, buzzing with science and chess clubs, team sports, and other extracurricular activities. Park-Rec also operated teams headed by coaches who expected you to show up, and gave you grief if you didn't.

Politicians at the time didn't call these kinds of programs "pork." They wouldn't have dared because working parents would have thought they'd lost their marbles. Everybody, from parents and educators to taxpayers and politicians, considered these after-school and summer programs to be a basic feature of a healthy community. In other words, they were an essential part of what intellectuals love to call the social capital of a civil society. Translated, that means communities couldn't get along without them.

Parents who worked knew instinctively that their children needed these programs. And so did neighbors and merchants, who were delighted to have the youngsters off the streets, out of harm's way, out of mischief, and in the hands of caring adults who were committed to their success.

Let me tell you what it really means to be a mentor or caring adult to a young person. Back in the mid-sixties when I was a law student in New Haven, Connecticut, I took a part-time job as a social group worker with teenage boys referred by the juvenile courts. To be perfectly frank, I needed the extra money to help support my wife and infant daughter. These kids were considered bad actors back then, although they certainly wouldn't be by today's standards. We met three times a week for several hours a day. We rapped endlessly. I'm going to date myself by reminding you that in those days, "rap" meant talking, not singing. We visited museums. We played basketball, and even competed in some Park-Rec leagues.

The boys and I really bonded and made a genuine commitment to one another. During the two years I worked with the group, not one of them got into any more trouble with the law whatsoever. Mind you, these were youngsters with long track records as juvenile delinquents. I learned a profound lesson about mentoring that I've never forgotten. One day I was late for my session with them because my class had run overtime. Boy, were they angry. They told me in no uncertain terms that the time we spent together at the time we were supposed to be together had become one of the most important things in their lives. They needed to know from me, right then and there, that it was the most important thing in my life and that I'd never be late again. I swore to them it was and I always made it on time from that day forward. At that moment, it became clear that the trusting relationship we'd built was what kept them out of trouble.

The point of this kind of youth work isn't just to keep young people busy, off the streets, and on the basketball courts. There's a connection between good after-school activities and solid academic achievement in school. High achievers routinely participate in a well-rounded array of activities after school, which encourages them to think and to learn. These programs give youngsters what one expert aptly calls a "mental workout."

Such programs contribute directly to academic success because young people get to practice skills learned in school. What kinds of activities qualify? Leisure reading, homework, constructive hobbies, activities in computer labs, exposure to the arts, stimulating conversations, extracurricular clubs, college visits, even organized sports and television in appropriate doses. In a successful Philadelphia program known by the curious name of Quop (for Quantum Opportunities Program), the youth worker checks every day on whether the youngsters he works with are actually attending school. On sunny warm days, he even checks twice, morning and afternoon, to make certain they haven't slipped out. As one Quop participant put it, "If he didn't see me for two days, [the youth worker] would go all over the neighborhood looking for me."

After-school programs like this can pay handsome dividends for the children involved and for society at large. Research shows that quality programs can raise math and reading performance, improve attendance, and reduce dropout rates. In addition, these programs often lead to improved behavior at school, better social skills, and higher aspirations for the future.

A big University of Florida study of 24,000 students in 1,000 schools across the country found that children who participate in adult-supervised extracurricular activities after school are more likely to graduate from high school than kids who spend their afternoons without adult supervision. Programs such as school bands, clubs, and sports teams enable students to form relationships with adults who help them grow up and who remind them regularly that school is important. A formal evaluation of Quop comparing the experiences of youngsters who participated with those who didn't found much the same thing. As *The New York Times* reported, the evaluation discovered that: "Of the 100 teenagers in the experiment, many more improved their basic skills, graduated from high school, and went on to college than . . . their peers. And they produced fewer babies."

That final sentence highlights another terrific benefit of solid after-school programs. Girls in the program got pregnant less than those who weren't in it. So besides helping youngsters do better in school, these programs also keep them out of harm's way. The afternoon hours from 3:00 until 6:00 P.M. are peak time for teen crime and sex. That stands to reason since when youngsters are adolescents, unsupervised idleness breeds mischief. The mischief teenagers come up with today makes my generation look like preschoolers. As Professor Milbrey McLaughlin and her two colleagues of Stanford University put it in their book, *Urban Sanctuaries:* "For most inner-city youth, especially young men, the time from early afternoon through late evening is spent in fierce communion with the streets." Study after study shows that active participation in after-school programs, even midnight basketball, curbs teen crime and pregnancy.

I saw these benefits up close when I worked with those supposedly bad boys back in law school. I witnessed it again many years later when I joined a men's organization called the Westchester Clubmen. It's a group of African-American professional men who have put down roots in Westchester County, just north of New York City. When it came time for me to serve as president, I persuaded the guys to start a mentoring program for black boys in late elementary school and middle school who were struggling with life and in school. I knew from my earlier experience as a mentor that the schedules of our members were too unpredictable and demanding for the youngsters to be able to rely on meeting with any of us on a regular basis. So instead we reached in our pockets and put up our own money to pay for a program director and tutors who would meet with about two dozen youngsters for a couple of hours after school four days a week. It's fitting that this offshoot of the

Westchester Clubmen is called the Club. The program regularly offers tutorial and homework assistance, social skills training, organized sports, and other kinds of appropriate extracurricular activities. Staff members meet every month with the youngsters and their parents.

I'll never forget my first encounter with one of the young men, Devon, soon after we started the Club in the fall of 1992. I entered a meeting room at the White Plains YMCA, which hosted the program. Devon was slumped in a chair, half asleep. I tried with some difficulty to strike up a conversation with him. Finally, in response to a question about what he had done lately in class, he mumbled that they were talking about the South Central Los Angeles riots and that he was supposed to write some kind of newspaper article.

I told Devon that I had once been an editorial writer with *The New York Times*. His eyelids opened slightly. I then engaged him in a conversation about what an editorial is. By then he had propped himself up from a 30-degree to a 45-degree angle. Next, I invited him to construct the essential components of an editorial—what comes first, second, and so forth. What would be the major points he would want to make? Whom would he want to talk to for background information? What arguments would he present? How would he analyze and articulate the pros and cons? Where would he come out?

By this time, he was sitting bolt upright, wide awake, playing journalist. We had connected; his mind was fully engaged. This young man started doing much better in school. Two years later, when I ran into him, he walked right up to me with a big smile and a hearty handshake. It was I who was proud to shake his hand. Going on ten years later, a woman came up to me in a Barnes & Noble bookstore near where I live. She introduced herself as Devon's mother and asked if I remembered him. I said I did. Bursting with pride and smiling broadly, she told me that he'd just finished the third year of college and planned to become a physical therapist.

Devon's success is just the beginning of the story. Listen to this. Ninety-eight percent of the 62 youngsters served since the Club was founded have graduated from middle school, even though most of them had said before entering the program that a high school education was not a high priority for them. More than three-quarters of them have continued to pursue their education after graduating from high school. The combined grade point average for the 21 boys enrolled in the Club in the spring of 2001 was B! What's even more heartwarming, a third of the youngsters made the honor roll during that marking period and they actually tutored other participants.

That's the impressive pay-off from solid after-school programs. These youngsters are a living testament to what African-American boys who weren't doing well can achieve academically when they are given encouragement, moral support, and reliable mentoring, along with a steady diet of academic reinforcement.

## BEYOND THE CLASSROOM

Nothing is more important than the role that parents and caregivers play in loving and nurturing their children, and guiding them toward happiness, fulfillment, and success in life. Cultivating a thirst for learning and a commitment to academic achievement is key to realizing each of those goals. Youngsters need to know that the important adults in their lives truly believe in their ability and potential. Without programming them every waking hour, they also need to participate in constructive activities after school and over the summer in order to continue their education and development in ways that are engaging and enjoyable.

"Even good students can be at risk if allowed to go home alone," says community sociologist Glenn Israel, the lead author of the University of Florida study. "After-school programs in which caring adults offer a variety of activities will be helpful whether they are on school grounds or other locations such as a YMCA or a community center. These are places where adults can nurture children, model positive behaviors, and provide support they don't get if they go home and sit in a house by themselves. Our research provides concrete evidence to support the conventional wisdom that schools can't do it alone."

The good news is that more and more schools are offering programs for their students after hours. In 2001, two-thirds of school principals who were surveyed by the National Association of Elementary School Principals said they had after-school programs in their buildings. That's up sharply from only 22 percent in 1988. In addition, high schools, which had been reluctant in the recent past to offer such programs, are increasingly providing their students with programs that emphasize tutoring, mentoring, and homework assistance, in addition to the more traditional activities such as sports, chorus, and yearbook.

Even so, according to the Urban Institute, there are still about 4 million children in America between the ages of six and twelve who are spending unsupervised time alone caring for themselves after school. Often they are baby-sitting for even younger brothers and sisters. This situation is especially risky for very young children or for those who live in neighborhoods that pose other dangers as well, such as criminals, drug users, or abusive friends or family members who show up unexpectedly.

Parents and caregivers should use every tactic they can think of to support the academic progress of their children while helping them to mature and remain hopeful. Take advantage of every formal program and real-life experience in school and out, no matter how ordinary it may seem, to turn children on to the joys of learning and discovery. The simple conversation I had with that young man in the Club not only sparked his curiosity, but also turned our talk into a hands-on, real-life learning experience for the two of us. For this youngster, a seemingly routine chat with an adult who took an interest in his schoolwork—and in him—became a logical extension of what he was doing in class. It can be as easy and as spontaneous as that.

When you're shopping for an after-school program, it's important to remind yourself that not all children are the same. "Choosing after-school activities for kids can't be a one-size-fits-all decision," says Karla Ballard of the National Urban League Young Professionals. "Young people have different personalities and interests. You should know who your children are, what they like to do, even what they dream of doing, then see what's near you that would fit their special needs."

Emma, a Boston dermatologist and the mother of two boys, can't agree more. "Enrolling my eldest in a local baseball league was one of the best things that ever happened to him," she explains. "When Ernie was in sixth grade, his grades started going downhill. I knew he loved all kinds of sports, so I figured I should get him involved with something he felt passionate about. His coach was a good, strong role model who demanded his players earn good grades and taught the team about the importance of self-discipline. After a while, Ernie's attitude began to improve and so did his grades." I'm sure that supportive after-school program contributed to the fact that Ernie is on course to graduate from high school with a B+ average and plans on applying to colleges and universities in the Boston area.

It wasn't so easy, however, for Emma to figure out what kind of activities her younger son might enjoy. "David never really liked sports and he is extremely shy and introverted," she explains. "One Sunday, after the church service, he surprised me by saying he would like to join the church choir. Now, he sings in both his school and church choirs, and his academic performance is even better than before. My boys are very different from each other and this is reflected in how they like to spend their time once they leave school. I've learned that what works for one doesn't necessarily work for another."

# YOUTH DEVELOPMENT PAYS FOR YOUNG PEOPLE, TOO

After-school programs matter to society because they help boost academic achievement by young people and curb their antisocial behavior. That's just the tip of the iceberg, though. These programs help youngsters grow up in a healthy way and avoid the temptations that get them into trouble. Broken homes are a regrettable but undeniable fact of life. In many families, both parents work, and more and more hours each day at that. When the federal government rewrote the welfare laws in the mid-1990s, parents were told they could stay on public assistance for five years tops. Then they had to leave and find a job. So the days of stay-at-home moms are a thing of the past in many households.

As a result, young people these days have lots of unsupervised time, which can be used constructively, mischievously, or worse. School-age children who have no adult supervision are prime candidates for gangs, which compete for their loyalty and time. Some years ago I was struck by the reason offered by a streetwise gang leader from Los Angeles on why young teens are attracted to gangs. "What I think is formulating here," he said, "is that human nature wants to be accepted. A human being gives less of a damn what he is accepted into. At that age—11 to 17—all kids want to belong. They are unpeople."

Well-run after-school programs compete with gangs to fill that dangerous void in youngsters' lives. *Urban Sanctuaries* describes some wonderful community-based youth development programs that are directed by individuals who are so dedicated and effective that the authors call them wizards. "It is important that inner-city youth have somewhere to go and something to do and crucial that those places and actions be positive," they write. "The young people we met came to the wizards' organizations in the first place because the places and activities looked like fun; they stayed because the organizations supplied a group and a purpose that meant something to the youth."

The authors interviewed many youngsters in these programs. "They told us: 'We know we're accepted here.' 'People care.' 'There's always someone to listen.' 'We're learning stuff for life.' The loneliness and suspicion of outsiders that the inner-city environment breeds into its youth also drives them to a place where they can belong. If that place is not a positive youth organization, it will be a gang. In fact, effective youth organizations look very much like gangs in the kinds of supports and recognition they provide to their members, but the outcomes of the two groups could not be more dissimilar. The gangs lead to violence, crime, and quite possibly death; the effective youth organizations enable youth 'to take a different road' that leads to life and a productive future."

To me, the testimony of young people is convincing evidence that these programs actually work. As one participant told the authors of *Urban Sanctuaries,* "[People in the organization] push me to stay in there and work harder. They know I can go all the way. I know I can go all the way. It's just a choice of me doin' it. I'm gonna get there." Naturally, youngsters are drawn to programs that combine education and fun. Asked why she participates, a youngster named Teri said: "Basically because they make the program so that it's fun. . . . If they're doing math . . . , they play math bingo or something like that. And I think that's fun for the kids because they don't feel that they're back in school again."

The key to good programs, say Professor McLaughlin and her coauthors, is good program operators who see potential, not pathology. "Therefore they design settings to guide youth through the mingled violence and indifference of the inner-city environment and to engage them in the types of learning and experiences that will transform these adolescent boys' and girls' sense of their own abilities and expectations so that they can duck the bullet." Effective after-school programs share certain features, according to the authors:

- They have family-like environments in which youngsters are valued and the rules of membership are clear.
- Their programs offer opportunities for active participation and

pose real challenges that produce accomplishments that matter to young people as well as the larger society.

- They are youth driven and sensitive to youth's everyday realities, values, aspirations, and interests.
- These programs assume that youth are a resource to be developed, not a problem to be managed.
- They are sufficiently flexible and attuned to inner-city youth so they respond to the unpredictable crises and demands that arise in youngsters' lives. They recognize young people's need to be treated as adults while still being sheltered as children.
- They are genuinely local, operating within and through the neighborhoods, institutions, and social relationships that make up youngsters' everyday realities. As one youngster said, "To really get the respect, you have to understand the neighborhood [and not assume that youth with the] same ethnic background [will all be alike]."
- Much like families, they enable youth by challenging, prodding, nagging, teasing, and loving them, and by providing many opportunities for practice and experience.
- They reach out to inner-city teenagers with messages that they will hear even though many are alienated from mainstream institutions, resigned to dead-end lives, and suspicious of anything that purports to be good for them.

The benefits of solid youth development programs after school and over the summer are so abundantly clear that it's puzzling why every child in America doesn't have a chance to participate. Children in affluent communities have plenty of after-school choices. But many urban neighborhoods are youth development wastelands. No Boy Scout troops or 4-H clubs. No YMCAs any longer or Little League teams.

In the late 1990s, public support for these programs gathered momentum and the federal government put up more money. But the field remains underfunded and the programs always suffer when government budgets get squeezed by other priorities or by economic recessions. The result is what Jack Foley of Cal State Northridge calls "recreation apartheid."

Parents and caregivers need youth development programs as much as young people do. Don't let your elected officials at any level of government get away any longer with ignoring this critically important service for young people. Effective after-school programs help youngsters grow up and lay the foundation for academic achievement.

## WHAT'S A GOOD PROGRAM?

Formal education is the hub of academic achievement, but a hub must have spokes or else the wheel won't turn, much less head where you want it to go. Extracurricular activities and summer programs complete the cycle of learning and achievement, and are a critical part of a child's life. Young people become achievers thanks to the guidance they receive at home, the instruction they get at school, and the support that's provided in after-school programs.

Youngsters aren't the only beneficiaries by any means. Parents who work, and even those who don't but need a breather in the afternoon, also benefit. When our two younger daughters were in elementary and early middle school, both my wife and I were working. There weren't any after-school programs to speak of within easy walking distance of our house. Year after year we tried hiring college students to come by and be with them. That would work for several weeks on end. Then they'd disappear off the face of the earth. Or they'd call to cancel because they had term papers or final exams. It was always something.

After all those fits and starts, we finally gave up when we thought they were old enough to be home alone. So in the afternoon, they kept one another company at home. Despite our best efforts, our daughters became what's called "latch-key" kids. Fortunately they got along just great. But imagine how stressful it would have been if they hadn't. Everyone managed, but the arrangement worried my wife and me constantly. It obviously didn't help when one of the girls called my office to report that when they'd gotten home after school, there were signs that someone had broken into our house through the back door. That scared the life out of me and I rushed to catch the first train home, but not before I instructed them to leave the house immediately, go to the neighbor's next door, and call the police. If I recall, we went back to those college students even if they couldn't make it every day. But that's the kind of anxiety parents must cope with when solid after-school programs aren't easily accessible or affordable.

Safety is one among many concerns. Children who are "home alone" are more likely to watch television or hang out with their friends, than work on their homework or read a book. Good programs, on the other hand, provide enjoyable and exciting learning experiences in a structured environment with caring adults. They reinforce the schoolwork that children do during the day.

Yet the reality is that finding a reputable after-school program that suits your child's needs can be challenging and, at times, frustrating. In many communities, these programs have disappeared because government funding or other financial support has dried up. It's in your self-interest, as well as your child's, to join other parents in advocating that the schools offer extracurricular clubs and that local government, businesses, and foundations fund community-based after-school programs.

## CHOOSING A PROGRAM FOR YOUR CHILD

Choosing an after-school program should depend on your child's needs as well as your own. In shopping around, some of the things to look for are whether they:

- Specialize in one thing or offer a variety of activities. Either approach can work provided it's done well.
- Tailor their program to the age and needs of the children they serve.
- Use a fun, hands-on approach to learning.

- Offer activities that expand and enrich—but don't duplicate— what the children already do at school during the day.
- Feature a caring and consistent relationship between the children and program staff or mentors.
- Offer sufficient compensation and training to attract and retain qualified and committed staff members.

Many of the best programs for school-age children offer a combination of academic, mentoring, recreational, cultural, and civic activities. Other excellent programs focus on one area and do it superbly. Plenty of terrific extracurricular programs are run by public school systems. Alternatively, they could be offered in school buildings by youth service agencies. Park-Rec Departments are major players in many places. There's a whole other world of after-school programs out there that are operated by community organizations such as the Urban League, by YWCAs and Boys and Girls Clubs, by community centers and settlement houses, by churches and other religious groups, by fraternities and sororities, and by civic clubs and mentoring organizations such as Big Brothers/Big Sisters.

Enlightened colleges and museums often get into the act. For several years I served on the board of trustees of Cooper Union, a wonderful college in New York City that focuses on art, engineering, and architecture. But that isn't where its mission ends. Cooper Union opens the doors of its studios and labs to schoolchildren who participate in an impressive array of enrichment programs during the academic year and over the summer. Similarly, other universities across the country operate summer camps that concentrate on a particular course of study, such as music, art, or entrepreneurship.

The military is also among the players in providing after-school alternatives for children. For instance, the Massachusetts National Guard and the Springfield Urban League team up in the summer to send some fifty youngsters in the eighth and ninth grades at the New Leadership Charter School to spend two weeks at a "Careers in Aviation" program. The children don't merely explore careers;

they actually pilot airplanes—under supervision, of course—and earn credit toward their pilot's license. Their stay on the campus of Westfield State College helps demystify college life and builds confidence that they'll be able to handle college when their time comes. Thanks to this summer enrichment experience, Springfield youngsters who probably doubted they could fly have discovered they can touch the sky.

After-school and summer programs take many shapes and cover a wide array of topics. They tend to fall into one of the following categories:

### 1. *Academic Programs*

Some programs make no bones about emphasizing academics. That's their primary reason for being. Take the Club in Westchester County, New York. "Our members felt that black men were becoming an endangered species and we had to reach the boys at this important age," says Cary Smith, a retired assistant principal at the White Plains Middle School, Highland Campus, and a Westchester Clubmen member. Mr. Smith works with the 25 young boys in grades six through eight enrolled in the organization's "Higher Aims After-School Tutorial Program" (that's what the academic component of the Club is called) located at the middle school. Students are selected from teachers' and guidance counselors' recommendations.

"Three to six P.M. is the most important time for at-risk kids," Mr. Smith explains. "In the program, teachers say to students: 'I'm here to help you, but you have to show me how you need help.' We concentrate on their weaknesses and what they don't understand. Most important, we show the young boys that if they have a dream, it can be obtained, that their hopes can indeed become a reality but not without working hard."

Derek Cradle, a social studies teacher and program facilitator for Higher Aims, says the program provides children with a structured environment that combines educational, social, and recreational components. "We give them tutorials in math, social studies,

English, and computers, as well as classes in conflict resolution and peer mediation," he explains. "And of course, time to play ball or work out."

Mr. Cradle reminds us that finding the after-school program that's right for your child is not always that easy. "A good program should be an extension of what's provided in the school," he advises. "Children should have the opportunity to express their talents, creativity, and skills. They should look forward to attending, and feel safe once they're there."

Here's a typical weekly schedule for the Higher Aims program. It'll give you a good idea of what a solid after-school program should look like.

- **Monday, 3:15–4:15 P.M.:** Math tutorial, social studies tutorial, special education tutorial; **4:20–5:20 P.M.:** Computer training in computer lab.
- **Tuesday, 3:15–4:15 P.M.:** Social studies tutorial, English tutorial, individual tutorials; **4:20–5:20 P.M.:** Recreation and sports, such as basketball and weight training.
- **Wednesday, 3:15–4:15 P.M.:** Group discussion—conflict resolution, goal setting, socialization, and peer mediation; individual tutorials; **4:20–5:20 P.M.:** Recreation and sports.
- **Thursday, 3:15–4:15 P.M.:** Social studies tutorial, English tutorial, individual tutorials; **4:20–5:20 P.M.:** Recreation and sports.
- **Friday, 3:15–5:20 P.M.:** Trips.

Children must be allowed to be children. It's healthy for them to play with friends and participate in activities just for the sheer fun of it. I firmly believe parents should resist any temptation to overprogram their children with highly structured, academically oriented activities every waking hour.

Nevertheless, parents should also make a point of enrolling their youngsters in some after-school activities that promote high achievement and provide academic enrichment. In *Beating the Odds:*

*Raising Academically Successful African American Males*, the authors describe how parents went about creating their own enrichment program for their scientifically gifted son because his teachers held such low expectations for him.

"The problem that we had was that our son was always big and they expected big black boys to be dumb jocks," his parents said. "So we had to create an atmosphere where he could do science and math outside of school. He participated in programs at the science museum in Baltimore and the Smithsonian. He participated outside of the school system and it was up to us to make sure he knew about those programs and would go to them."

2. *Summer Programs*

After-school programs aren't just limited to the school year. What children do during their summer vacation also plays a role in their path to academic achievement. In fact, students from low-income families tend to slip backward academically over the summer. Wealthier kids tend to keep moving forward over the summer because they're more likely to attend camps and enrichment programs, visit libraries, and take family vacations where they learn something new.

"My mother really wanted me to go to the summer science program for high school students at Berkeley," says John, now a senior at an Oakland, California, high school. "She nagged me, tried to bribe me, just bugged me until I gave in. My mother knew that I was good in computers, and she just didn't want me hanging out all summer on the street. She was right—I learned a lot and met some really good people. One of my teachers there is helping me get into Berkeley when I graduate high school. It's like I already have a mentor before I even start college."

3. *Cultural Programs*

After-school programs that emphasize music, dance, drama, painting, writing, and other artistic endeavors are an important part of a child's development. Unfortunately, some parents consider these activities "fluff," and even a waste of time. The truth is that many children are gifted in these areas, and after-school programs that nurture and support their talents can create a sense of confidence and self-esteem that young people can carry over into their academic life. Sometimes youngsters find out what really makes them tick and discover their life's work in these programs. I'm told, for instance, that the celebrated artist Jacob Lawrence learned how to paint at an after-school program in Harlem.

"My daughter's grades in school actually began to improve after she started taking ballet lessons," says Kim, a government worker from Washington, D.C. "She became more focused and motivated. Then she developed an interest in music and asked to take flute lessons. With her musical gifts came a higher aptitude for math. She now tells me that if she can't be a dancer, she wants to be an engineer!"

Janie Victoria Ward, author of *The Skin We're In: Teaching Our Children to Be Emotionally Strong, Socially Smart, and Spiritually Connected,* says that even though cultural programs are very important for a child's development, some African-American parents may be reluctant to engage in certain activities with their children—such as visiting museums and libraries, attending lectures, and plays—because the parents feel those activities are "too white."

The trouble is that this type of reluctance can shortchange your children, stifle their interests, and stunt their growth as capable and curious young people. As Ms. Ward says, "If you are a black adult for whom crossing over feels dangerous, you may choose to stay put, even at a cost to your children. It's not that blacks don't see the value of these cultural activities, or that they are nonintellectual or anti-intellectual. It's just that for many, it feels too treacherous, too hard to be the first to or the only one.

"It's tough to be the only black eighth grader enrolled in an art class at the museum or in a swimming class at the YMCA, especially if your black peers are not supportive; and it can be hard as well for the parent who stands by waiting in a crowd of all-white parents. Parents need to take a deep breath and dive in, summoning their courage and maintaining an unwavering focus on the good that can result for their children."

## 4. *Sports Programs*

Sports are equally important for boys and girls. Team sports teach teamwork, naturally. Youngsters learn to cooperate with one another to accomplish a common goal that they couldn't reach on their own. Coaches are among the best mentors because they set high expectations, create a shared stake in success, instill discipline, enforce rules, and command respect. Besides, in more and more schools, students increasingly aren't allowed to compete in scholastic sports unless they maintain a prescribed grade point average.

"My coach believes in me," say Sara, an eighth-grade soccer star at her suburban Atlanta school. "She urges me to do my personal best, yet calls me when she thinks I haven't practiced enough or am not putting in everything I have. But I like that she wants me to do better all the time. If she has confidence in my ability, then I don't want to disappoint her." Sara's nine-year-old brother Raymond likes basketball and she's urging him to go to basketball clinic after school. "It's different just shooting hoops with your friends than learning how to be part of a team," she says.

Recreational activities help develop young people's physical skills and channel their energy in constructive directions. They also teach them the importance of getting along with others. Academics should not be sacrificed for sports, however, so make sure your children don't place athletics above achievement. Like many an impressionable youngster, I used to dream day and night, in school and out, of becoming a major league baseball player. I just knew I'd make it. A love of sports actually can help in school if it inspires youngsters to read, as I did, everything they can about their heroes and favorite teams and if it inspires them to learn math by understanding, for example, how sports statistics are calculated.

Parents must constantly remind their children that the odds of ever becoming a professional athlete and earning a decent living at it are minuscule. You don't want to throw cold water on their dreams at a tender age. But please don't allow them to slight their studies because they're under the illusion that they'll reach the NFL or WNBA. When I discovered around age 14 that I couldn't hit a curveball for the life of me, I thanked my lucky stars that my folks had always insisted that I take school seriously, just in case. Father knew best, maybe because he couldn't hit a curveball either when he was a kid.

## TIPS ON FINDING QUALITY PROGRAMS

How should you go about choosing a solid after-school program for your child? Start by doing some homework on who's out there operating good programs. Ask other parents and friends in the neighborhood whether they are aware of any. Solicit leads from the teachers and principal at your child's school. Check with the local school board, youth bureau, or Park-Recreation Department about available programs in your community. See whether there's a Boys or Girls Club, YMCA or YWCA, settlement house, or community center nearby or within easy commuting distance. If there's an Urban League in your community, call them for suggestions and leads. Find out what your church or other churches have to offer. Contact the library, local museums, and various cultural institutions to inquire if they sponsor after-school programs.

If there doesn't seem to be much available, you may need to join forces with other parents to urge your school board and mayor to fill that void in the children's lives by instituting some after-school programs in the community. Should that fail, the fallback may be that parents with the resources and time could start some on their own. I realize, though, that's really burdensome and probably unrealistic for many parents.

Once you track down some names, you'll want to check out the programs. Call them to see what they offer and when. Pay a visit someday when they're in session. Get a list of all of their program offerings by age group and subject matter so you can see which are suitable for your child. Pick the particular ones that catch your eye. Find out how much it would cost to enroll your child and decide whether that's in your price range. Then sit in and observe what the children are doing and whether they appear to be stimulated and engaged. See whether the children respect and obey the staff. Are there any signs of disciplinary problems because some children act out too much, or because the staff isn't skilled enough to handle active and inquisitive youngsters?

Solid after-school programs share some pretty common characteristics. I would urge you to look for those that offer:

- Instruction that is tailored appropriately to each age group. This should take into account the different developmental stages children go through as they grow up.
- Hands-on learning experiences that stress active, indeed interactive, participation, such as computer instruction, cooking lessons, and science experiments.
- Tutoring that gives children time to complete their homework and offers focused instruction in subjects they need extra help with.
- Community involvement that presents children with opportunities, say, to volunteer at senior citizen centers or help clean up city parks. This teaches young people the importance of giving back.
- Sports and artistic activities that provide outlets for physical and creative energy and teach teamwork. This allows for the expression of more than just academic skills.
- Enriching field trips to plays, city parks, places of business, television and radio studios, newspapers, downtown business districts, art and science museums, concerts, planetariums, houses of worship, and even other neighborhoods. This broadens children's horizons and exposes them to the richness of American society.

## FORGING AHEAD

As parents and caregivers, we should see to it that our children receive the attention, support, and direction they need. When we're home after work and on weekends, that's our role. But when we cannot be with them, then we should make certain a caring adult is.

Some families can afford this on their own. But others simply cannot because they don't earn enough to pay the fees. In that case, I firmly believe that the government should fill the void, whether it's the school system or the Park-Recreation Department. That's the way it was when I was a child heading off to Raymond Playground nearly every day after the last school bell rang. City officials in those days wouldn't dare question the wisdom of providing these programs or mess with the appropriations that paid for them.

Sadly, after-school programs can fall victim to budgetary tugs-of-war today. When I was human resources administrator for the City of New Haven in the late 1970s, we funded after-school programs for kids and centers for senior citizens. A decade after I'd left the job and moved to the New York City area, I was invited back to New Haven to deliver a speech. At the time, youth violence was plaguing the community. Adults were terrified of the teenagers.

At one point in my speech, I posed a question to the audience. I asked whether the after-school programs we'd funded were still in place. The answer was "no," I was told, because the city was too broke. There'd been sharp cutbacks in municipal spending to cope with the recession. I then asked whether the senior citizen centers were still there. The answer was "of course."

Just as I'd suspected. This emboldened me to ask the uncomfortable question about local priorities. What was more important to the quality of life and the future of New Haven? The after-school programs that promote the healthy growth of teenagers and take them off the streets? Or senior citizen centers that enable the elderly folk to socialize and pass the day? I knew that question about spending priorities would annoy the audience, but I asked it anyway to demonstrate how adults decide, time and again, that the needs of kids are expendable in a crunch. That's morally wrong and it's just plain dumb as far as I'm concerned.

Well-run after-school programs benefit youngsters in so many ways that participation should be standard operating procedure for all children as they grow up. Think of it. They offer academic enrichment, improve social and interpersonal skills, connect children with caring adults such as mentors and coaches, and offer a safe haven for young people who'd otherwise be home alone or hanging out on the streets. That's a return on investment that Wall Street would envy.

# CHAPTER SEVEN

# Computer Literacy
# Matters, Too

No one ever accused me of being a "techie." We bought our kids some of those gadgets that were all the rage in the 1970s. Remember the Atari video game machines that you hooked up to the television? I am proud to say that I didn't fall for every advertisement touting the latest toy, especially once I noticed that we'd barely broken in one machine before it was proclaimed obsolete by commercials hawking the new, improved version. The replacement cycle for this stuff barely outlasted my fast-growing children's shoes. If a TV could last ten years, I grumbled, why couldn't the video game machines that were attached to them?

I had another brush with technology when I worked as an editorial writer for *The New York Times* in the early 1980s. The newspaper automated its entire word-processing operation. So we all started using computers to compose our articles and editorials. On Friday, the routine in our department was to write the editorials for Saturday, Sunday, and Monday. That way, barring a big breaking news story, we wouldn't have to work over the weekend. More times than I care to remember, we'd be close to done late in the day when the entire system would crash without warning, totally wiping out three days' worth of writing. This was infuriating and frustrating. But it was totally our fault in the final analysis. Why, you might ask? Because few of us had bothered to understand the mysterious ways of computers. In other words, we weren't pressing the "save" key as we went along. After several crashes, we finally learned the first lesson of using computers.

My technological illiteracy continued in my next career as a senior VP at Channel Thirteen in New York City, the nation's largest public television station at the time. I ran the division that produced all the notable series that the station produced for PBS, acclaimed series such as *Great Performances, Nature, American Masters,* and *Childhood.* My impressive title didn't mean, though, that I'd suddenly mastered technology. I'll never forget a visit by some producers who came to show us their wares. Not one of the station vice presidents in the room, starting with me, knew how to operate the VCR when our visitors asked us to pop in their tape so we could screen it!

So you see, I can testify firsthand that technology can be intimidating or off-putting for adults. But that's no reason to deprive our children. We must grin and bear it, then get our children onto the Information Superhighway.

By the time I took over as president of the National Urban League in 1994, I at least knew how to talk the technology talk, even if I still only half-stepped the walk. When I was touring the League's headquarters, I discovered to my astonishment that we still used a printing press to crank out meeting notices. Even I knew that was ancient technology.

So I declared to my Urban League colleagues one and all that we had to gear up to enter the twenty-first century, technologically speaking. Since then, we've progressed from relying on that dusty printing press to web-casting major events at our annual conference. Of course, I still don't have a clue about what kind of stuff we had to buy in order to get from there to here. I just knew where we had to go and that we'd better get there quickly. It was a matter of survival and competitiveness for our organization.

The exact same is true for our children. They, too, must be technologically literate in order to prosper in the Information Age economy of the twenty-first century. This point was really driven home to me at a breakfast meeting with Dan Carp, CEO of Kodak. He helped me see the direct connection between literacy, technology, employability, and economic competitiveness.

Mr. Carp explained that pretty soon Kodak's factory workers would be required to use wireless hand-held computers that store all sorts of information about inventory supplies and assembly procedures. To use these computers, employees must be able to read. But this goes way beyond identifying the words in front of them on the screen. They must be able to follow the instructions, proceed from one step to the next, and find solutions to the problems put to them by their supervisors. So word recognition and reading comprehension are critically important.

Applicants who possess what's now seen as basic skills can qualify for good-paying jobs as twenty-first-century factory workers. Those who don't might be lucky enough to land a lowly job as a twenty-first-century janitor. Kodak's very success in a global economy depends as never before on a workforce that can read and is technologically literate.

Take another example—telephone operators today at the Educational Testing Service, the outfit that designs the SAT and a host of other qualifying exams. On the day the results become available, anxious test-takers call in from all over the world to find out how they did, what to do if they were disappointed, and when they can get another shot at taking the exam. Telephone operators who field these calls must dive into their computers, dig up the desired information, and handle follow-up requests. All this in a calm and considerate voice so they don't alienate their customers. Again, technological literacy is required for tasks that once were pretty routine and required minimal educational skills.

Candace Smith, the 32-year-old Atlanta attorney who sits on the National Urban League's Board of Trustees, understands this firsthand. "The influence of technology on our lives is totally unlike what our parents experienced when they were growing up," she says. "It's not only the computer and Internet; it's the videos, the music, the immediate exposure to a more multicultural and global society. The world is constantly shifting, and when it does, we know about it right away. There's no lag time. As a result, our priorities are different—we don't necessarily want to be tied to one organization or company but be more independent and on our own. We can't be afraid of change or we'll be left behind."

So whether you're comfortable using computers or not, every adult who is raising a child needs to understand that traditional literacy and technological literacy are closely intertwined in this day and age. Computers with Internet access should be as commonplace as books and beds, telephones and TVs. You know that famous slogan for the American Express card: "Don't leave home without it." Well, when it comes to your kids and computers: "Don't let them live in homes without them."

## COMPUTER JITTERS

Michelle Price is a communications consultant, a volunteer at the San Diego Urban League, mother of two, and grandmother of one. She has three words to say to parents and caregivers who are afraid of technology and computers: "Get over it!"

"All parents must learn the basics, which include word processing, e-mail, and the Internet," she says. "Trust me, there's nothing overwhelming about it. The Internet was developed to retrieve information and communicate more efficiently. What it does is connect and strengthen the community, only faster, cheaper, and more far-reaching than the telephone and the mail."

Michelle became a converted "techie" in 1988 when she was working for the University of California and wanted to move up from her position. She started learning about computers on her own, motivated by the bottom-line fact that she knew she could earn more money if she mastered the required skills.

"I wasn't afraid," she says. "In fact, I was curious. I regard technology like this: I'm going to master it; it's only a machine. We all use technology all the time. No one is scared to use a cell phone or CD player, right? But you need an incentive to learn computer skills—and what's a better one than knowing you'll be able to help your kids."

Michelle relates how one day she was at the checkout line in the supermarket and overheard a discussion between two young women in their early twenties. "They were talking about how they earned so little in their sales positions at a large clothing chain store. I kind of put my head into their conversation and asked them why they didn't learn computer skills. I told them they most likely would be able to find a job at a salary higher than they were getting now.

" 'I'm scared I would fail a computer course,' one said. 'I'm embarrassed I would look stupid,' said the other." Michelle says she can understand why many African Americans like these young women probably don't have enjoyable recollections about school, and have no desire to go back to the scene of the crime, so to speak, to repeat an unpleasant experience. But she urges them—and others like them—to get over this defeatist mind-set that limits their possibilities.

"If you don't learn about technology, you won't be a participant, you won't be a contender, you won't even be in the game," she advises. "You'll be relegated to pushing a broom and one day they'll even have a robot for that!"

As I mentioned earlier, I didn't exactly embrace the computer like a long-lost friend either. If you're like me, it makes you nervous facing a machine that occasionally acts smarter than you, talks back to you, breaks down unexpectedly, and sometimes even does things you didn't tell it to. Using computers isn't always a piece of cake, especially for adults who aren't accustomed to them. But this I can tell you: Children take to technology like ducks to water. Don't deprive them of it just because you are hesitant to get wet yourself.

Modern technology empowers people to educate themselves at their own pace and up to their individual potential. It equips us to obtain information and acquire knowledge on our own, without asking permission. It's human instinct for adults to want their children to enjoy a better life than they had. Technological literacy is one key to realizing that dream. In the twenty-first century, cyberspace may be the only integrated neighborhood in the galaxy.

## COMPUTERS IN SCHOOLS

Given their role, schools have every reason to be wired. Unfortunately that isn't the case across the board. According to research conducted by Project 2000 of Vanderbilt University, even though about 70 percent of schools in this country have at least one computer connected to the Internet, fewer than 15 percent of classrooms have Internet access. Not surprisingly, schools in poor, minority communities trail affluent ones in getting wired for the Information Age, just as children in low-income minority families are less likely than youngsters in well-off families to have computers with Internet access at home. These gaps hold youngsters back because it means they're deprived of an educational tool that's getting more important with each passing day.

On the bright side, parents and young people, educators and community groups like the Urban League aren't taking this so-called "digital divide" lying down. They've become increasingly resourceful about how to close it. For instance, youngsters attend after-school programs at the League's "digital campuses," where they are tutored using high-tech software. They seek out computers at churchs, libraries, and the wired homes of their friends.

A little-noticed resource for instilling computer literacy is your local library. Libraries do wondrous things for children and with children, but they're pretty low key when it comes to letting the world know about it. Don't let that dissuade you from checking out what they have to offer. The fact of the matter is that 95 percent of the 16,090 public libraries and branches across the country now offer computers with Internet access to the public. Your taxes make it possible for libraries to exist. Take full advantage of every service they have to offer you and your children.

Some schools are beginning to equip every student with a

portable computer to use at school and at home. According to *The New York Times,* "For years, technologically inclined educators have been pushing this approach—often called one-to-one computing—as a radical way to provide Internet access and word-processing programs to students any time, anywhere." With the advances in wireless networks and the cost of laptops dropping to $1,000 or less, the individual laptop movement in schools is beginning to grow. A school district in New York City expanded its laptop program to include 4,500 students. And more than 800 schools and 125,000 students nationwide are taking part in Microsoft's "Anytime Anywhere" learning program, which the company started with Toshiba in 1996.

Robbie McClintock, director of the Institute for Learning Technologies at Teachers College, Columbia University, believes that taking a laptop home every night is extremely beneficial for students. "This moves the education program from the school into the students' hands on a twenty-four-hour basis," he says. "Yet, ultimately, the value of technology education is up to the teachers. The experience can be very good or it can be like wheeling a VCR into the classroom and turning it on."

The "digital divide" holds teachers back along with their pupils. Teachers in schools serving mostly minority students are less likely than educators in predominantly white schools to use computers or the Internet during instruction in class. The same pattern is true of teachers who teach low-achieving vs. high-achieving students. Many teachers say they would like to integrate more technology into classes for lower achievers, but the realities of teaching them make it difficult. *Education Week* reports that some teachers feel they have to forgo technology to make sure they cover the prescribed curriculum, which is a more time-consuming task with students who have weaker skills or less motivation.

"It takes longer to put technology into a lesson," says James L. Smith, chair of the Minority Leadership Symposium for the Internal Society of Technology in Education based in Eugene, Oregon. "Schools targeted for poor performance are dealing with other issues. Technology is last on the totem pole."

Since I've never taught so much as a day in a K–12 school, let alone one serving low achievers, far be it for me to second-guess teachers who say it's a struggle trying to incorporate technology into instruction. But I do know this: The less educators use tools like technology that help close that *Preparation Gap* and *Achievement Gap,* the faster and wider these gaps grow. It's a fact that schools serving affluent students generally use technology in more intellectually powerful ways, such as teaching students how to make presentations, analyze information, and express themselves in writing. By contrast, teachers in schools serving low-income students are more likely to use computers to emphasize skills reinforcement and remediation. These schools must break out of this confined instructional box in order to unleash every child's potential, regardless of their ethnicity or upbringing.

"I wish there were more technology training and computer work in my school," says Willie, a fifth-grader at an overcrowded Chicago elementary school. "I'm so happy when I can spend time on the computers, but there's always other kids waiting to use them. I try to go use the one at the library, but there's always a line there also. If there were more computers at school, I would go on the Net during my lunch hour or after school before the bus comes. At home, my neighbor on the third floor has a computer she sometimes lets me use, but only when she and her kids don't need it."

Installing and using technology in schools takes money, of course. States and school districts that are strapped financially are often tempted to place school computers on the budgetary chopping block first. Still, as Clint Stables, assistant superintendent of schools in the rural Virginia district of Northumberland County, told *Education Week,* "If you make technology cuts, that will disproportionately affect poor kids. Technology is not a luxury item," he added. "It's a necessary part of every kid's education if he or she is going to compete in the global economy."

If our children don't have regular access to computers in school, it will be tough for them to acquire the technological skills necessary to compete in America's twenty-first-century economy. Every classroom across the country should be outfitted, wired, and actually plugged in. School officials like to claim they are up-to-speed. But parents should make certain those PCs aren't stored somewhere in the original boxes, gathering dust.

## COMPUTERS AT HOME

"My five-year-old son came home with an assignment that required our sitting down at the computer together and working on letters of the alphabet," says Charles, a hospital administrator from Houston. "I'm lucky that I bought a computer recently, but what about families who don't own one?"

Having computers in the home is essential these days. It's not enough for youngsters to use them only in the classroom. Why? Because they can do their schoolwork at home whenever they want and don't have to travel or stay out late to use one. Studies conducted by the Digital Divide Network, sponsored by the Benton Foundation (www.digitaldividenetwork.org), show that home computers actually motivate students to do their homework. A home computer also gives parents the opportunity to become involved in their children's homework and see what they're being taught. Teachers in some schools even use computers to communicate with parents about what's happening in class, how their children are doing, and how parents can help out on their end. In addition, home is where family members can spend as much time as they want on computers, surfing the Internet, digging out information, or playing educational games. Libraries and community centers don't allow unlimited use, for understandable reasons.

Home computers and Internet access don't come free of charge. For families struggling to meet the bare necessities of life, this can be a stretch. Fortunately some groups have devised some imaginative approaches to help them get on the Information Highway. One example of this is Computers for Youth (CFY), a nonprofit organization based in New York City that provides inner-city students and their teachers with fully equipped home computers at no cost, and follows up with comprehensive services including training, technical support, and web content. The organization was founded to refocus digital divide efforts in the home environment.

In 1999, CFY selected a middle school in the South Bronx and provided all the students, parents, and teachers with a Pentium computer after they had completed a half-day training session. All the computers came with Internet accounts that CFY covered for the first three months. Afterward, the families had to pay $8.50 a month. When the families and teachers took their computers home, CFY continued providing them with technical support free of charge.

The impact of CFY's program is encouraging. In a study published by the Digital Divide Network, the computers were shown to have a positive effect on academic performance of the students who participated. They used their computers for homework, word processing, and finding information on the Internet. This helped them organize their schoolwork better and they enjoyed doing research on the Net. It showed in classroom performance. Teachers reported that these youngsters' schoolwork improved in terms of presentation and quality. They also said their pupils thought "more clearly" when writing on the computer. Students whose parents didn't allow them to hang out on the streets after school said that using the Internet kept their children from feeling too isolated socially.

By now you're probably wondering what angel enabled CFY to pull this off at so little cost to families. The answer is so simple yet creative that it probably can be done in communities all across the country. Here's how it works. Local businesses donate used computers to CFY, which the organization then refurbishes and upgrades before distributing them to families. Once the computers are taken home, many families buy additional bells and whistles for them, such as printers, scanners, or educational CD-ROMs. This shows they really value those PCs and find them useful. The program has been so successful that CFY is expanding it to additional middle schools in low-income New York neighborhoods.

"Public policy to close the digital divide must also focus on bringing technology into homes," writes Elizabeth Stock from Computers for Youth. "We must strengthen the home-school connection, enable students and teachers to use technology in intellectually more powerful ways, and encourage parents to become more involved in their children's education. It is school and family together that instill in children the knowledge and skills to lead productive lives. Let's not leave the families behind."

Baltimore is home to another effective program that's placing computers in the home. In this case the families live in the Terraces complex at the Edgar Allan Poe Homes, a public housing development in the Maryland city. The housing complex was built with high-speed Internet connections for the purpose of creating an "electronic village," which would allow residents to communicate easily with one another and the world beyond their complex. Residents who complete a free 20-hour basic computer course get a certificate of computer literacy that entitles them to a free Dell computer, fully installed in their apartment. These computers are supplied as an appliance and do not become the residents' property.

"The program is intended to boost some of the nation's poorest people into the rich universe of opportunity represented by computers generally and the Internet in particular," writes Francis X. Clines in *The New York Times*.

Constance Mayfield is the executive director of the Noah Group, a private community service organization administering the program at Poe. "It's a generational thing," she says. "Some kids are already being taught computers in school and so they want them at home. But they have to convince their parents to take the classes."

Residents of the housing project clearly get the point of the program—and of computers. Take Charnita Johnson, an unemployed mother of two. She says she is taking the course "for the kids and to get the certificate. Kids need a computer for their future so I just decided I'm going to get this!"

Poe Learning Center is an old power plant in the public housing complex that has been converted to classroom space. Teenagers use the computers there for a nine-month course sponsored by Cisco Systems, the giant Internet company. Designed to expose these young people to careers in technology, the course has already routed scores of them into jobs in the computer industry at $30,000 a year and more.

To my way of thinking, home computers rank right up there with refrigerators and stoves as the most important appliances for the home. Computers nourish your children's minds, while the other two help nourish their bodies. As competition in the computer business heats up, prices of PCs keep plunging. That's a great deal for families, if not for the manufacturers. Remember, in order for you and your children to stay connected, you must be connected.

## WHAT CAN PARENTS DO?

Except for folks in tough financial straits, there isn't much excuse any longer for families to go without computers. If buying even a rebuilt one is out of reach for a family, then the next best thing is to make darned sure your child gets access to one at school, in a community center, or through a special program like those I described. My main point is parents and caregivers shouldn't rest until their youngsters get regular access to a computer.

If you're like me, in the beginning the idea of learning how to use a computer is about as enticing as undergoing root canal or mastering the VCR. But believe me, it isn't so bad and it's actually loads of fun once you get the hang of it. Besides, I believe every parent and caregiver has an obligation to get comfortable with computers because you should set the example for your children by owning one, using it, and showing your children how to do so along with you.

Remember—computers and the Internet go hand in glove. A computer without Internet access is little more than a glorified word processor. A computer coupled with the Internet is an electronic magic carpet that can transport you and your child on journeys of discovery into cyberspace.

You don't need a Ph.D. or a certificate in computer programming to make your home computer-friendly for your kids. Here are some practical suggestions from experts like San Diego communications specialist Michelle Price and other experts about how to help your children become computer literate:

1. *First, find some free computer training.* Before you spring for a home computer, take a lesson or two on the job or at an adult education center. That way you can begin familiarizing yourself with this new world of technology. There are more programs that offer free or low cost computer training than you might think. Find out the location of your nearest community technology center by going to the library or checking out www.digitaldividenetwork.org or www.ctcnet.org. An instructor can show you how to access these websites and then enter your zip code to look for free computer centers in your area that offer classes for novices and more advanced continuing education lessons.

2. *Make a firm commitment by getting a home computer.* You can ask advice from your instructor as to the kind of computer you need. If you can't afford a home computer or Internet access through your TV, use a computer in the library and ask for help by checking out www.ctcnet.org, which lists computer recycling centers where you can get free computers.

If your children are old enough, have them help you purchase a computer, printer, software, and whatever else you need and can afford. Get them to do some research about what kind of computer will work best for them, will be compatible with their school or work after school, and will grow with them as their technological skills grow. Go to computer stores together to check out different models. Make the purchase of a computer an important learning experience for each of you.

3. *Plunge into computers with your child.* Earlier in this book, I said the best way to get your children started on reading is to start out reading to them and with them. The same is true of launching them on the path to computer literacy. They'll play if you will. After all, most youngsters take to technology with ease. They just love gadgets such as Etch-a-Sketch and video games. They aren't afraid of new things. In fact, they delight in switching roles and teaching

their parents a thing or two. Many a time I was totally flummoxed by the VCR, especially that 12:00 on the clock that blinked constantly, only to have one of my kids stroll into the room, notice my frustration, and patiently instruct me on which buttons to push.

Take an interest. For example, if your son plays computer games all the time, go online with him and have him explain what kind of technology he's using and how his favorite game works. That way, you are both teaching and encouraging one another. If the computer is just too much of a mystery for you, however, invite a friend over to help out. You can use the opportunity to learn along with your child.

4. *Master the fundamentals of computer literacy.* There's no question that navigating computers takes some skill and curiosity. We can't all be experts at it, let alone know how to solve mysterious malfunctions or search and destroy computer viruses. However, there are some minimum computer literacy skills every youngster should acquire, such as:

- Activating the computer and performing basic functions, such as word processing and, as I learned the hard way, punching the "save" button frequently.
- Accessing the Internet and understanding how to explore various websites.
- Using the Internet to dig up information and data, and to do research for school papers and personal use.
- Utilizing e-mail to communicate with other people.
- Composing Powerpoint presentations.

5. *Weave the computer into everyday life.* You and your children can use the Internet to find the best shopping values, look up sports results, check out movie schedules, and make travel plans. The more you use it—even for recreational purposes—the easier it gets. A computer can be used in the privacy of your own space, at your own pace, at any time—after school, after work, when you can't sleep at night, when an event you planned has been canceled be-

cause of inclement weather. We're all busier than ever before. Once you get the hang of it, a computer is truly a time-saver.

6. *Create your own home page for free.* A home page is a great way to interact with your children, and it also serves to keep everyone connected. You can post photographs of your family, write up funny experiences, and list important dates such as birthdays and anniversaries. Check out www.blackplanet.com, which is directed to the African-American community. It shows you how to create a customized home page at no charge. Plus it offers free e-mail.

7. *Advocate for more computers in the schools and libraries.* The more computers your child has access to, the better. It's an investment that just keeps paying.

The bottom line, as San Diego's Michelle Price reminds us, is this: "It's never too late—or early—to learn. My 20-month-old granddaughter Shalice is already on the computer. She has been imitating my daughter and me since she's been 11 months old and is now really beginning to learn. It's all about exposure. My mother took my family to museums, on trips. She read to us constantly. She showed us that there were other people and places than the ones we were familiar with. That's what the computer does today: it's the modern window to the outside world."

Technology is truly liberating. It empowers us to gather information, explore new terrain, accumulate knowledge, and communicate at will with others. Some people think of cyberspace as virtual reality. That's fine, but I have a far less cosmic view of its importance. I see it as an essential part of the foundation for academic achievement and intellectual growth. After reading, 'riting, and 'rithmetic, computer literacy must come next for our kids, even if it doesn't start with R.

# CHAPTER EIGHT

## *Demanding—and Getting —Good Schools*

So far I have focused primarily on what parents and caregivers should do at home to help children become high achievers. And on where you can turn in your community for inspiration, assistance, and support. I realize this is hard work and you have to keep at it. But children don't raise themselves. Ready or not, willing or not, that's the job we signed on for as parents and caregivers. We owe it to our children to give them nothing short of our very best shot.

This isn't your burden to bear alone, however. The schools they attend shoulder a huge responsibility for making sure your child learns and achieves. That stands to reason since the classroom is where formal instruction occurs, where subjects such as language arts and science are taught, and where academic skills are nurtured. So unless you're one of those rare parents who's into home schooling, the teachers and principal in your child's school must uphold their end of the education bargain.

Many public schools work quite well. My guess is they're mostly in the suburbs where life is good and parents are pretty well educated themselves. Some elite public schools perform off the charts, largely because they get to choose who goes there based on the children's academic credentials. Some schools in low-income and

working-class communities are solid. A few exceptional ones perform what to outsiders probably look like miracles given the odds
their pupils face.

But the picture of public schools in inner-city neighborhoods,
aging suburbs just outside, and impoverished rural communities is
by and large pretty bleak. For years skeptical experts said little
could be done about it. Even so, some pioneering school reformers—such as Dr. James Comer, Ted Sizer, and Ronald Edmonds—
and scores of determined teachers and principals refused to throw
in the towel and write off poor and minority youngsters who tend
to live in these low-performing school districts. For the sake of the
children, I'm thankful these reformers, renowned and anonymous
alike, soldiered on with their education experiments. That's because
over the years they've shown there are instructional approaches and
ways of managing schools that enable poor and minority children
to learn and achieve at high levels. The bottom line is it can be
done.

Many educators do what's right because it's the right thing to
do. But the sad reality of human nature is that oftentimes it takes
concerted pressure to get grown-ups to do what's right. That's why,
as conscientious as you are on the home front, you also have to stay
on the school's case about making sure they educate your child—
and every child—well. As an advocate, you shouldn't focus solely
on your child. If you don't join forces with other parents to improve
the school overall, you could find yourself solving a problem in one
grade or with a particular teacher, only to find yourself dealing with
the same frustrating issue the following year.

It's worth repeating the point I made earlier about the way the
U.S. labor market works in this day and age. Remember I said that
85 percent of all jobs today are skilled or professional positions.
Young people without much education have little prayer of qualifying for these jobs.

# WHAT WORKS

Believe me, it doesn't have to be that way for your children. When I read *Education Week* or look over the reports of the Education Trust, a research and advocacy outfit focused on elementary and secondary schools, I see there are hundreds, perhaps even thousands, of high-performing public schools serving poor and minority youngsters all across the country. Many of them even outshine suburban schools on state tests. In addition to the attributes listed on page 127, these successful schools also:

- Use high academic standards to design their courses, assess their students, and evaluate their teachers.
- Invest heavily in professional development so that their faculty stays on top of their game and focuses on teaching methods that help their students meet tough academic standards.

That's why I tell everyone the evidence is clear that urban principals and teachers know how to create schools that enable youngsters to achieve at very high levels regardless of where they live, what their race is, and how much their parents make. So if your child's school performs miserably year after year, get impatient. Get angry. Get involved. Insist on answers or demand alternatives.

I'm sure you won't be alone in your dissatisfaction. Find other parents who feel the same way, then join forces with them to pressure the principal, the superintendent, the school board, and the state commissioner of education to improve the school's performance. Stay with it until you accomplish your goal, namely high-quality education for your child and the other children in your community.

That's what parents and community leaders did in Mount Vernon, a suburb north of New York City with all of the economic and educational challenges of a big city. The school district there is predominantly black, and 60 percent of the students are poor. For decades, the schools had been considered failing, with fourth-grade reading scores among the worst in the state. In 1998, just one-third of the fourth-graders in Mount Vernon met the state reading standards. In one particular school, only 12 percent of the students met the state standards.

The school board seemed content to accept the status quo. So did the school administrators, teachers, parents, and the larger community. And this went on for years. But then something happened. A group of adults in the community refused to accept any more excuses for school failure, and mobilized to turn around the school system and save their children.

Local community activists, led by a couple of Urban Leaguers who have been involved in our Achievement Campaign, got absolutely fed up. The Rev. Franklyn Richardson (a former trustee of the National Urban League), Ernie Prince (head of the Urban League of Westchester County), and other leaders from the African-American Leadership Forum of Westchester County organized black parents to vote out the old school board and elect a new one.

That accomplished, the new school board fired the old superintendent—who had been there for 25 years—and hired an energetic and determined new school superintendent named Ronald Ross. A former teacher and principal in New York City and Hempstead, Long Island, Superintendent Ross became the first African American to head Mount Vernon's schools in the city's history. The school district includes 10,000 students and has a yearly budget of $114 million.

Backed by a mobilized and energized community, Superintendent Ross wasted no time in administering a strong dose of reform medicine to the school district. To begin with, he declared that the era of accepting excuses for the failure of poor and minority children to achieve was over. He warned teachers that there was room in Mount Vernon's schools for only two kinds of teachers—those who genuinely believe all of the school district's children can achieve and those who act convincingly as though they believe it. If they don't fall in either category, he warned them bluntly, then they should find another career or else they'll be removed from the classroom. They got the message.

"I am in public schooling, and I have no control about which students walk through that door," Superintendent Ross says. "I have to teach them, no matter who they are. But I can have some control over the teachers. We had to change the culture, and that's what we did," he explains. "We can always make excuses for why students in a district like this don't do well. But we are not here to make excuses."

Superintendent Ross hired literacy expert Dr. Alice Siegel to zero in on reading. Together, they told the principal and teachers of every elementary school that their main job was to make certain their pupils become good readers. He hired staff to relieve school principals of mundane administrative assignments such as monitoring lunchrooms or making sure children catch the school bus at the end of the day. That freed the principals to observe classes and talk to teachers.

Some central office administrators were let go and the money was used to hire instruction coordinators in English/language arts and six other subject areas emphasized by the state. The educators devised a new curriculum that standardized what should be taught grade by grade. This included district-wide lessons, right down to the work that students in each grade would take home on weekends. Teachers' schedules were rearranged so they'd have time to work at least once a week with their principal and a reading specialist. The specialists began visiting every classroom every day, to help out, and observe.

From day one, parents were an essential ingredient in Mount Vernon's recipe for academic success. As partners in the reinvigorated educational enterprise, they took on such assignments as monitoring their children's homework and verifying in writing that their children were reading at least thirty minutes at home every night, as required by the school. To encourage students to read on their own, Superintendent Ross challenged them to read fifty books a year and rewarded those who did with a bicycle. He also firmly believes that youngsters who don't write on a regular basis aren't likely to read well either. So the schools got students to write every day and then talk about their written work in class.

Superintendent Ross scorns the idea of teaching to the test so children can pass it. His view instead is that if schools teach youngsters to read books that stretch their vocabularies and reading comprehension skills, they'll do just fine on the state reading exams. Makes perfectly good sense to me. Plus, as you'll see below, his approach really works.

So, Mount Vernon teachers were given ambitious goals along with firm instructions and intensified support on how to reach these goals. For their part, the teachers demanded higher performance from their pupils, while at the same time instilling confidence in them that they could succeed.

The Mount Vernon turnaround strategy worked swiftly, with striking results that delighted parents and stunned educators across New York State. Listen to this. In 1999, 35 percent of Mount Vernon's fourth-graders read at or above the state standard. The next year that jumped to 51 percent. In 2001, the percentage of fourth-graders meeting the state reading standard soared to 77 percent. That's easily the fastest and steepest climb I've ever heard of.

Some Mount Vernon schools with mostly low-income students actually showed more than 90 percent of their pupils at or above the state reading standard. This exceeded several school districts in Westchester County that are much wealthier. That isn't the end of this heartwarming story. In 2001, Mount Vernon had three of the most improved schools in New York State. Several of its schools more than doubled the ratio of students passing the state reading test in three years. In one school, the percentage of students who passed soared from 21 percent to 60 percent.

The Mount Vernon success story shows that children achieve at high levels when they are challenged academically. And that principals and teachers can perform at high levels when they're told in no uncertain terms that's the name of the game and then given the professional support that enables them to succeed as well. School reform takes hard work and common sense, that's for sure. But Mount Vernon shows that it's not rocket science. Skeptics say Mount Vernon is such a small school system that its approach wouldn't work in big-city districts. That's baloney. Just divvy up the school district into manageable clusters the size of Mount Vernon and drive reform the way Superintendent Ross did.

Parents and community groups who see that the schools are coming up short year after year should mobilize, as they did in Mount Vernon, to demand that school boards and educators dramatically improve the schools. And that they do so with dispatch, not at a snail's pace. It took Mount Vernon only three or four years to turn things around, so it shouldn't take other school systems forever.

When public schools let children down year after year, then I think you are entitled to run out of patience and insist that the district transfer your child to a stronger public school. If the school turns a deaf ear to your pleas and remains mired in failure, I for one cannot blame you if you join the call for school choice, at least until school boards, administrators, and teachers unions get the message that the schools had better shape up or else your children will ship out.

Mount Vernon is a wonderful example of what can happen when parents, community leaders, and educators get on the same page about academic expectations for children and then implement the instructional practices in school and support mechanisms at home to help youngsters meet the loftier standards. The perennial challenge, there and elsewhere, is to stay the course so the schools don't revert to business as usual. As educators in Mount Vernon can attest, that isn't as simple as it sounds, so parents and community leaders must stay alert. When it comes to ensuring that your children achieve, perpetual vigilance is the name of the game.

## Raising the Bar for Public Schools

Research and practical experience show that black children can achieve on par with other children when the education they receive is on par as well. *U.S. News & World Report* published a series of instructive articles in its October 9, 2000, issue on public schools that have experienced dramatic turnarounds. Perhaps not surprisingly, they used a pretty similar recipe to improve student performance: committed parents, students, community leaders, and educators working together to define the problem, devise solutions, and implement change.

One of the myths that has undermined school improvement efforts—and thereby limited the potential of millions of children—is the view that differences in children's academic performance are primarily due to differences in their innate ability to learn. Educators may join the chorus in saying all kids can learn, but experience shows many of them believe otherwise. Teaching children who present lots of challenges is hard work and can wear educators down. As a result, some teachers who toil year after year in schools filled with low-achieving minority pupils may come to expect less of their students.

Mount Vernon's Ronald Ross refused to accept defeatist thinking from his principals and teachers. And look at the remarkable progress he delivered in three short years as the result. "All children, no matter what their color or background, can achieve in public schools," he asserts. "There's nothing wrong with public education except the leadership that underestimates our young people."

Academic failure is no longer an option for our young people. "The battle for civil rights was fought in the streets; the current battle will be fought in the classrooms," says Eleanor Horne, vice president of the Educational Testing Service and a trustee of the National Urban League. "We have to make sure that we shape the battle and stick to it to the end. At stake are the very lives of our children."

## SCHOOL IMPROVEMENT AGENDA

Children are entitled to the best education possible. It's our job as parents and caregivers to do our level best to get it for them. Of course, we can't all afford pricey prep schools for our kids. Many families cannot even handle tuition at parochial schools. That's why for the vast majority of American children, public schools are the only game in town. The fate of your children hinges on how well their schools perform.

The good news is that more and more schools are getting the job done, not only for the few, but also for most of their students. The fact that these effective schools exist and that they're growing in number removes any lingering excuse that educators may offer for the inability of urban and rural schools to equip poor and minority youngsters to achieve at grade level or better in core subjects such as reading, writing, and mathematics.

The sorry fact, though, is that all too many inner-city and rural schools that serve low-income and minority youngsters leave much to be desired. The teachers are overwhelmed and the students are performing below par and way below their potential. Things must be shaken up for the sake of the children. And it's up to parents and community leaders to do the shaking until educators and boards of education get the message. That's what got the ball rolling in Mount Vernon. Even if you're satisfied with your child's school, don't become complacent because the school could slack off once you take your eye off what's happening there and how it's doing.

I've watched various school improvement initiatives over the years. There are several common principles that strike me as key to success. These can guide how parents go about pressuring politicians and educators to improve the schools:

1. *Insist on no-nonsense leadership.*
Low-income and minority children often are caught in a trap between lofty standards and lousy schools. Politicians like to say that public education is a local responsibility. That's fine, but the fact is

the state government sets the academic standards that students must meet in order to graduate. And even though U.S. presidents and members of Congress talk a lot about improving public schools, the federal government doesn't put up nearly enough money to wipe out the gaps between wealthy school systems and financially strapped school districts in such critical areas as teacher quality, school facilities, and technology.

"I have an unwavering belief that all children can learn at the highest level, but we have to be prepared to take risks to reform the system and make it happen," says Ernie Prince, president of the Urban League of Westchester County. "Standards and testing are important—if you don't keep score, you're just practicing. In order to meet these standards, however, changes have to take place not only in our schools but also in our communities at large."

Risk-taking requires risk-takers. In my view, that's what leaders are supposed to do. In the case of children and achievement, the leaders who must step up to the plate are all those "education" presidents and governors and mayors, those legislators who pass laws, state education commissioners, school board members, school superintendents, principals, and teachers. They must make the policy decisions, allocate the resources, make the hard choices, and focus as never before in order to make all the schools work for all the children.

That's what Superintendent Ross set out to do in Mount Vernon and look how quickly the school district produced results, and dramatic ones at that. Anything short of exerting that kind of leadership sells your children short. Parents should mobilize to send politicians and educators a crystal-clear message that if they don't take risks for children, their own careers are at risk.

2. *Start educational accountability with the educators.*

Accountability is a two-way street. It begins with the adults who run the schools and the parents who rear the children. It ends with children themselves, who'll enjoy the benefits of solid academic preparation or else pay the ultimate price of failure. Kati Haycock, head of the Education Trust, goes right to the heart of the issue of where accountability belongs. If students fail, she observes, "There are already serious consequences for the kids, but not for the adults."

State education agencies oversee school districts, but until recently they've ducked responsibility for the schools' performance. Locally, school boards, administrators, principals, and teachers, protected as they are by union contracts and tenure, have side-stepped accountability as well. Academic failure by low-income and minority students was explained away by the fact their families were poor. Or what's worse, by scientifically discredited and down-right racist theories that African Americans are inferior intellectually.

After two decades of promising school improvement experiments, these excuses by the adults who preside over public education no longer hold water. The hundreds of examples of high achievement by low-income and minority children confirm that they will meet society's expectations of them, if adults will meet their obligations to them.

To begin with, state education agencies should shine a bright spotlight on how well individual schools do in lifting the achievement levels of minority children who lag far behind. School-by-school report cards are one effective way to do this. Public exposure helps jolt educators out of their complacency.

The chain of command in local school districts starts with boards of education that set policy and pick superintendents. At least that's what they're supposed to concentrate on. In many communities, though, school boards get all caught up in micro-managing the system, dispensing patronage, and harassing superintendents instead of supporting them. They seem to focus on everything except student achievement.

When elected school boards come under fire because their schools are failing badly, they often defend themselves as the democratically chosen voice of the people. But many a lousy school system is presided over by an elected board. My advice is to be wary of automatically defending them if they aren't getting the job done for the children. Accountability is accountability, and I don't care whether a school board is elected or not, or for that matter, what its racial makeup is.

The key issue is whether kids are learning what they should and meeting, or better yet, surpassing the academic standards imposed by the school district and the state. If the school board in your town tolerates failure year after year, then vote them out of office. If that doesn't work, then petition the governor to take over the school system, or empower the mayor to place the schools under mayoral control. When it comes to school boards, "If you aren't part of the solution, you are part of the problem." Either the school boards become obsessed with raising student achievement or else they should step out of the way.

The next piece of the puzzle is finding a superintendent of schools whose primary mission is promoting learning and ensuring that all children achieve. It's fine to boost the performance of youngsters who already are excelling. The truest test of a superintendent in my book is whether youngsters who are tuned out start tuning in, whether they acquire the fundamental skills they need to keep moving forward, whether they perform up to their potential, and whether they pass the gatekeeping exams that entitle them to advance from grade to grade and ultimately graduate from high school, fully prepared for the future. Lift the bulk of students who lag way behind, who read "below basic," who face being held back in grade—that's the charge school boards should give the superintendents they choose.

Obviously superintendents should endeavor to keep the school buildings in good shape, make certain books reach the classrooms, maintain harmonious relations with the unions, and avoid operating deficits. But if the academic performance of low achievers doesn't improve on a superintendent's watch, then I believe that education leader will have failed the test of accountability to the constituency that matters most—the children.

To illustrate how what I'm talking about plays out in the real world, let's return to Mount Vernon for a moment. There the local school board had been firmly entrenched for years. Its all-white members didn't represent the parents and students of the district, the majority of whom are African American. In order to break the school board's hold, the black community had to put their individual differences aside and unite behind its slate of candidates.

"In 1996, we organized and educated our constituents for the purpose of electing African-American representatives to serve on the school board," says Rev. Franklyn Richardson, pastor of the Grace Baptist Church in Mount Vernon. "We still lost, and once again the school board remained one hundred percent white. So we went back to the drawing board. What could we do differently in the next election?"

Rev. Richardson and other leaders of the black community in Mount Vernon were determined to break the hold of the city's powerful school board. They analyzed the election results, and saw that each of the winning candidates had received roughly 5,000 votes.

"So we would get 6,000!" Rev. Richardson says. "We mobilized our volunteers on a block-by-block basis. Community and church leaders, parents and concerned citizens, all worked together to pull out the vote. And in 1997, every one of our candidates won. We started out with five African Americans out of nine elected to the school board; now the board is one hundred percent black."

But as Rev. Richardson is quick to point out, "It ain't over yet!" He explains: "Our challenge now is to move from revolution to governance. We must work to change the mind-set of people who are used to fighting the system so they can become managers of a system whose primary interest should be empowering the community."

One of the first items on the newly elected school board's agenda was to hire a new school superintendent. The search committee nominated Ronald Ross, and the rest is history. "I consider what I do as a calling, not a job or profession," says Superintendent Ross. "I plan for the future, but live for the day. Excellence is caring; it's making the special effort to do more. And it's not just about money, although greater financial investment in our children would certainly be welcome!"

If the schools continue to struggle, then even more drastic measures than those imposed in Mount Vernon may be necessary. Some teachers and principals don't belong in these schools in the first place. There could be many reasons for that. They're out of steam. Or they aren't certified, nor did they major, in the subjects they teach. Or deep down, they don't really believe poor and minority children can achieve. Whatever the reason, they should be retrained, encouraged to leave, or, if need be, dismissed.

Many states and school districts put failing schools on a watch list that's akin to probation, and require them to implement improvements. They're treated like other bankrupt but salvageable enterprises. Remove the principal and assistant principals, replenish the faculty with capable and committed replacements, and institute a recovery plan.

Students who are stranded in schools that are beyond revival should be free to enroll in other public schools, in charter schools, or in other alternative public school settings more suited to their unique needs. That's what Florida did and it has spurred some schools to improve. The ultimate sanction for failing schools is to shut the doors, which school districts have done.

True accountability can make life uncomfortable for educators. But lousy education is calamitous for children for the rest of their lives. That's why parents should insist that education accountability start with the educators.

3. *Professionalize the teaching profession.*

Without good teachers, there won't be good schools. It's as simple as that. What teachers know and can do is the most important influence on what students learn. Jared, a ninth-grader from Cleveland, Ohio, got it exactly right when he said: "The most important thing is to have a teacher who goes the extra mile for you. It makes you feel so not alone. You know someone cares about you and wants you to do good."

Tens of thousands of well-qualified and highly motivated teachers do a marvelous job in schools that serve urban and rural children. But the undeniable reality is that the schools with the lowest scores on the state exams have the highest percentage of uncertified and unqualified teachers.

Black children, for instance, are held to the same high standards as other children. But the schools that serve them frequently lack teachers who are certified in math and science. One-third of math teachers and roughly half of physical science teachers in middle school and high school didn't major or minor in the subjects they teach. Often "the most senior teachers opt for the nicest schools, while we put our weakest teachers in the hardest locations," says Robert T. Jones, president of the National Alliance of Business. These schools pay their teachers less than those in the suburbs. They're short on motivated teachers who believe that all children can learn, and typically are located in very large and impersonal buildings.

If we want good teachers for our children, we must pay teachers more in order to attract more qualified people into the profession. It certainly makes no sense for school districts facing the biggest hurdles to pay their teachers and principals less than nearby districts where the challenges aren't as formidable. Parents need to tell the politicians and school boards that they firmly support competitive salaries for educators. In fact, I happen to think that starting teachers with master's degrees should be paid about the same as young MBAs, attorneys, and engineers.

"Two years of a bad teacher will generally destroy a child in public education for the rest of his or her life," Superintendent Ross says. "Teachers have to be committed above all. They have to like kids and believe in them. They have to put in that extra effort, take that extra time. And they can't just teach to the test—that's the quickest way to fail. Kids walk out of the classroom learning nothing but the test."

As we all know, a good teacher can make all the difference in the world. They can shape our future and inspire us to make our dreams a reality. The late Nobel Peace Prize winner Ralph Bunche never forgot the life-shaping influence of his sixth-grade teacher Emma Belle Sweet.

"She taught me many things, and especially geography, in that large class in the old Fourth Ward School in Albuquerque, now long since destroyed by fire," recalled Dr. Bunche. "But nothing could be so important to me and of such enduring quality as her simple, human act of figuratively leading me gently by the hand to a sense of self-respect, dignity, and worth."

4. *Provide challenging courses for all children.*

"The simple fact is that students, poor and rich alike, learn to high levels when they are taught to high levels," writes Eleanor Dougherty and Patte Barth, senior associates at the Education Trust, in *Education Week*. "Yet, poor and minority children in this country are systematically bludgeoned into low academic performance with a steady dose of low-level, boring, if not downright silly assignments and curricula."

How can our young people possibly meet tough academic standards when they're routinely excluded from rigorous courses geared to those standards? According to the Education Trust, high-scoring white and Asian students are twice as likely as high-scoring black and Latino youngsters to be assigned to college prep courses, who are, in turn, tracked disproportionately into basic and special education courses.

Parents shouldn't stand for this kind of discrimination. Insist that a school explain the full array of courses it offers. Inquire about the entry requirements. Schools tend to offer rigorous courses, such as honors and Advanced Placement, to youngsters who earn the highest grades and test scores. That doesn't mean they're the only pupils who can handle the work in those courses. It's more like a reward. I understand that, but it ignores the fact there are plenty more children in the school who aren't being challenged or educated to their full potential.

The battle I'd urge parents to wage is to persuade the principal and teachers to greatly expand the number of slots in academically challenging courses. Some parents will raise concerns about lowering standards. I believe that's a bogus objection. What's really at work is elitist thinking that if too many students get to take these courses, they're no longer exclusive enough for their kids. Don't fall for that line of argument. What you're after is the best education possible for your child and for all children who tend to be short-changed by the schools.

"We must stop sorting kids into bins of winners and losers," warns Ernie Prince of the Westchester Urban League, "because whenever a sorting bin exists, it's always our kids who are sorted out."

Some studies suggest that the majority of courses in many inner-city schools are dumbed-down versions of the curriculum taught to students in affluent suburban schools. Data from national exams in reading and math also indicate that African-American and Latino students are less likely than white students to be taught reasoning skills and are more likely to be given worksheets—considered a low-level activity—in class.

Parents can force the issue—and they should. "Parents should be prepared to go as far as they can when advocating for their child," advises Anna, a seventh-grade English teacher in Denver who is also the mother of five. "Be prepared to listen to your child's teacher, but don't be afraid to question what you're being told. It's not always the child's fault. Find out why the school wants to put your son in special ed or says your daughter doesn't qualify for Advanced Placement courses. Believe me, external pressure works— I know that from both sides of the desk."

Unlike students in suburban schools, poor and minority students have a "steady, unrelenting diet of mind-numbing assignments in all subject areas," according to Dougherty and Barth. In a study they conducted, they uncovered a number of glaring weaknesses in the way schools in low-income communities work, such as:

- Grades are based on process, not product. For example, if students turn in a paper neatly produced on a computer, they'll get a higher grade regardless of how their work addresses the subject.
- Assignments rarely ask for research or accompanying documentation and citations.

- High school students are routinely given babyish assignments.
- Topics for assignments are shallow and don't require complex thinking.

Parents should be on the lookout for these practices that go with lousy schools. If you spot them at your school, then join forces with other parents to insist that the school get serious about the quality of education it offers.

## What Parents Can Do

Entrenched bureaucracies sometimes change out of enlightened self-interest. In other words, they see the light and reform themselves before it's too late, before a more compelling alternative becomes widely available. Other times, it takes concerted external pressure to force bureaucracies to change—for the sake of their "customers" as well as themselves.

For far too long, public educators have kept their heads in the sand, like ostriches, in the face of an urgent need to improve urban and rural schools. Parents, politicians, and business leaders have grown restless with the sluggish pace of school improvement. I urge parents, caregivers, and community leaders to keep up the relentless pressure to create straight "A" schools for your children and for every American child. Make no mistake. The Mount Vernon success story would not have happened if the "villagers" had not banded together and made it their business to insist that the young people of the village receive the education they deserve.

Even parents in comfortable suburbs must stay right on the school's case. "I made an assumption that in suburbia the school would place my child where she needs to be," says Marie, a stay-at-home mother from a well-to-do community in New Jersey. "We moved here from Brooklyn where my daughter, Taisha, was in an overcrowded, understaffed kindergarten class. One of the reasons we moved to this town was for its highly rated school system.

"When Taisha was in third grade, the school sent me a notice that she was reading and doing math at an eighth grade level. I called her teacher and asked him if there were any special classes my daughter could take at the school that would encourage her academic talents. He said, 'Oh well, we do have a gifted and talented program.' I didn't receive that call—I made that call! My daughter was testing in the 90th percentile nationally, and if I hadn't found out on my own that she was eligible for advanced classes, she would never be there now."

So regardless of where you live and what your family circumstances are, here's what you must do in order to make sure that your children are well served by their schools and placed squarely on the path to academic success:

1. *Be vigilant.* Make it your business to ask your children what's going on at school. Look for possible trouble spots such as teachers' negative attitudes, tracking, discipline problems, safety issues, and so on. Stay in touch with your kids and pay attention to what they are telling you—and keeping from you.

2. *Be informed.* Educate yourself about what your children are learning in school and what the school offers. Find out if the work they're doing is grade level or better and whether it meets the academic standards imposed by the states. Familiarize yourself with the standardized tests your children are expected to take, when they must take them, and how they should prepare properly to do well on them. Superintendent Ross has the *parents* of fourth-graders actually take the state reading exam from the prior year so they'll better understand what their children are expected to know for the exam. Read up on national and state educational policies and regulations, with an eye to how they will directly affect your children.

3. *Be involved.* Join the PTA. Attend parent-teacher conferences and "meet-the-teacher" nights. Vote in the school board elections—remember Mount Vernon—and maybe even run for a seat on the board yourself. No one can fight harder than you for your children's right to a good education.

4. *Be vocal.* Speak up if you see a problem with your child's schooling, even if you think there may be repercussions because of your activism. Go to your child's teacher or principal if you detect unfairness in the way your child is being treated. If you feel you— or your child—are being punished for your outspokenness, contact your pastor, the local Urban League, or another community-based organization.

5. *Be visible.* Make sure the school knows that you are actively involved in your child's education. Become involved in the governing process of your local school system. Attend school board meetings and get to know your local elected representatives.

6. *Organize.* Meet with other parents to discuss how you can work as a group to help your children. Start on a grassroots level— with neighbors, relatives, friends. Many voices are stronger than one, and work in unison to ensure that achievement matters as much to your children's school as it does to you.

"Parents must be advocates for their children in school, in the community, and sometimes even within the family," advises Dr. Freeman Hrabowski in *Beating the Odds: Raising Academically Successful African American Males.* "It is the parents' role both to stand up for the child and to hold the child accountable. . . . Parents must also coach their children through their development. An effective coach teaches concrete skills, pushes an individual to achieve full potential, and is consistently supportive, win or lose."

Children want to do well. When large numbers of them fail, it's because adults—school administrators, teachers, parents, and their larger community—have failed them.

We all know it doesn't have to be this way. Lousy public schools can be turned around if the adults mobilize to do so; if adults will say: no more excuses for school failure. I'm not downplaying the problems that many schools and the families they serve face. Just the opposite. While these problems may not go away, they needn't defeat the efforts of determined parents and educators to close the *Preparation Gap* and ensure that children achieve, regardless of their family circumstances. That's the moral of the Mount Vernon comeback and of the inspiring turnaround stories in urban and rural schools all across America.

# CONCLUSION

## *Our Collective Responsibility to Make Sure "All the Children Are Well"*

It is said Masai warriors in Africa greet one another with the words: *"Eserian Nakera."* The lyrical phrase means: "And how are the children?" The traditional response is: "All the children are well."

The transformation of American public education will be complete when the schools embrace that Masai saying—in word and deed. Millions of young people are doing the right thing every day. It is up to us as parents, caretakers, and concerned members of the community to take collective responsibility for our children's destiny and do everything in our power to equip them to become high achievers. Nor can we ignore youngsters who've never gotten on the pathway to academic success or who've strayed off course. The slogan of the Urban League is *Our Children = Our Destiny.* That means all children, not just some of them.

As a parent or caregiver, what should you want the schools to provide your children by the time they graduate from high school? How will you judge whether they're getting what they need along the way and by the time they graduate from high school? That's an interesting and important question. One place to look for an answer is those academic standards that school districts and states are imposing.

There's another way of framing an answer that may be useful

and relevant. When I posed this question to myself, I got to thinking about the kinds of skills I've needed throughout my career, as well as my life as a husband, a parent, and a citizen of the United States and the world. Here are the skills and competencies I've utilized over the years:

1. *Literacy*—easy command of reading, writing, and speaking in English. Although I don't have a working knowledge of a second language, that certainly would be helpful from this day forward.
2. *Mathematics*—workable command of the basic computational skills required in the workplace and everyday adult life, from balancing a budget at work to a checkbook at home.
3. *Reasoning and critical thinking*—capacity to ferret out information, find answers, and solve problems. Employers increasingly expect workers to be innovators and problem-solvers. The days of people earning a decent living by working mindlessly on assembly lines are numbered.
4. *Science*—appreciation of the nature and uncertainties of the scientific inquiry. This is especially critical as health care assumes greater importance in our personal lives and as we're called upon as citizens to understand threats such as chemical warfare.
5. *Citizenship*—understanding of the primary historical, cultural, demographic, political, and economic forces and values that have shaped this country. Appreciation of America's relationship to the rest of the world, as well as the major forces shaping other nations and cultures.
6. *Computer literacy*—everywhere we turn, technology is transforming the way we work, the way we learn, the way we play, and the way we communicate with one another. There's no avoiding it, so we'd all better get with it.

I believe every youngster should emerge from high school with these six skills well in hand. That means it's the job of schools to make certain all children acquire these skills. And it's our job as parents, caregivers, and members of the village to make certain the schools do their job. Beyond these basic competencies, the remaining courses that students choose should be shaped by their aspirations and ability. Young people who are headed straight for the labor force may opt to specialize in certain workplace skills suited to their interests, while college-bound students could elect more advanced academic courses that equip them for higher education.

Even in the nineteenth century, as our ancestors clawed to freedom through tunnels, they reached back to help others who were following behind them. In the twentieth century, the so-called "talented tenth" and the faithful 90 percent took assassins' bullets and faced down Bull Connor's ferocious dogs so that the doors of opportunity would open for future generations—for today's generation—of African Americans.

Each one of us, from every walk of life, must enlist in the effort to empower our children to compete and succeed on a level playing field. If our ancestors, armed with hope and little else, could successfully withstand the monstrous oppression of slavery and later mount the ramparts of segregation, then surely the villagers of our generation can rally our collective energy and assets to propel the rest of our people into our country's economic mainstream. If we could create great universities and businesses right under Jim Crow's nose, then surely by working in concert we can make public schools work, and establish enterprises that prosper in our community and the broader economy.

"It's the circle that helps develop the child who must be told over and over again—and understand—that he or she is worthy," says Alexis Gabrielle, a parent ambassador with the New York Urban League's Standard Keepers program. This Brooklyn mother and grandmother devotes her time to reaching as many other parents as possible in the community to educate them about what they should know in regard to the academic requirements expected from their children.

"Helping one another should be part of our commitment to a young person's education," she advises. "The standards we set for our children, both at home and in school, will be upheld throughout their entire lives."

It warms my heart when I hear young people who really get the point of academic achievement. "The reason I want to do well in school is so that I have more choices when I get older," says 7-year-old Anthony, a first-grader from Birmingham, Alabama. "I want to keep going no matter what."

Back in the 1800s, homesteading offered Americans a chance for economic self-sufficiency by providing them with forty acres and a mule. Our collective task today is to give Anthony and all of our children the twenty-first century equivalent of homesteading—what one economist with a sense of humor calls "40 Acres and a Sheepskin."

Adults know there are no guarantees in life. But we also know from hard-earned experience that academic achievement gives young people their best possible shot at becoming victors instead of victims in the twenty-first century.

Parents and caregivers bear primary responsibility for rearing their children and making sure they receive a solid education. That goes with the territory, so to speak. But we mustn't let them shoulder that burden alone. You've probably heard the saying that "it takes an entire village to raise a child." But that's just flowery rhetoric unless we make it real. That's why it is our collective duty to make certain our children get the high-quality education they need and deserve. Then we, the villagers of America, can rightfully say: "All the children are well."

# ACHIEVEMENT MATTERS:

## Getting Your Child the Best Education Possible

## Hugh B. Price,
## President of the National Urban League

## ABOUT THIS GUIDE

The suggested questions are intended to enhance your group's reading of ACHIEVEMENT MATTERS: Getting Your Child the Best Education Possible. We hope the following questions will lay the groundwork for parents and caregivers to help their children succeed within the public school system and in life.

# READING GROUP GUIDE QUESTIONS

Chapter One: Taking Charge of Your Child's Education

1.  How can you help your children develop the actual reading and academic skills they'll need to do well in school? What can you do to encourage their enthusiasm about learning and inspire their love of reading at the earliest age possible?

2.  How can you keep a close eye on your children's teachers and schools to make sure they're providing quality education and preparing your children properly?

3.  Do you know what academic skills your children must have and what academic standards they must meet in order to advance from grade to grade and to graduate from school? Do you know what's expected of them at each grade level and, if not, how would you go about finding out?

Chapter Two: Spreading the Gospel of Achievement

1.  Do you think your children are put down by their classmates when they strive to do well in school? How can you overcome the negative peer pressure your children may experience if they are determined to be "smart" and do well in school?

2.  Who are some role models and historical figures that might inspire your children to achieve academically? Who influenced you?

3.  Are there any programs and organizations in your community that recognize children who achieve? If you aren't aware of any, how can you and other parents, community groups and school officials work together to recognize and reward

youngsters who want to do well in school so they don't
buckle under to peer pressure to slack off in school?

Chapter Three: Reading: The Bedrock of Academic Success

1.  What ways can you imagine using to communicate the joys
    of reading to your children and to introduce them to books at
    the earliest possible age?

2.  What kind of books and reading material do you feel are ap-
    propriate for infants? For toddlers? For young children, pre-
    teens and teenagers? What books did you love at these ages?

3.  Do you know how to—and take the time to—monitor your
    children's reading skills? If they slip behind, do you know
    how to find tutorial help for them at school and outside if
    need be?

Chapter Four: High Achievement Starts at Home

1.  What kinds of things can you do at home to show your chil-
    dren that reading and learning are really important to you?

2.  How can you show your children you support their academic
    efforts and are proud of their hard work in school?

3.  How can you nurture the determination to succeed academi-
    cally even if their schools aren't the best and their buddies
    aren't serious about doing well?

Chapter Five: Navigating the School System

1.  Do you know how well your children's schools are doing?
    How can you go about becoming more involved in parents'
    organizations and community groups that keep watch on
    your local schools?

2. Have you had any trouble dealing with your children's schools? What was the problem? What did you do about it? Were you successful or frustrated by the experience? Would you deal with it differently today?

3. How do you feel about charter schools? What about special education? What other educational "hot buttons" issues are you concerned about?

Chapter Six: Learning Isn't Over When the Last Bell Rings

1. Are your youngsters enrolled in after-school programs? Do the programs have a serious academic component, like tutorials and informative trips? Are you satisfied with these programs?

2. How do you go about deciding if your children are well served by these programs? What are you looking for from them?

3. How can you go about finding after-school programs for your children? How can you and other concerned adults in your community start one yourself?

Chapter Seven: Computer Literacy Matters, Too

1. How can you encourage your children to learn about technology and computers at the earliest age possible—even if you don't know much about computers yourself?

2. Do you have a computer at home? If not, why not? Do you plan to get one? If you do have a computer at home, how do you encourage your children to use it for educational purposes and not just for recreation?

3. Do your children's schools have computers and teach com-

puter skills? Are there after-school programs in your community that offer free training both for your children and yourself?

Chapter Eight: Demanding—and Getting—Good Schools

1.  How can you organize with other parents and local leaders,
    and advocate for good public schools in your community?

2.  What can you imagine doing at the classroom level, at the
    school level and at the school district level to help ensure that
    your children receive a really solid education? Do you know
    how to evaluate the performance of the teachers and princi-
    pal at your children's schools and of the school district over-
    all? Does the state or the school system itself issue report
    cards on school performance?

3.  Are the mayor, city council, state legislature and governor
    truly committed to providing high quality public education
    for all children and ensuring that all schools do a solid job? If
    not, what can you do about it and what will you do about it,
    for the sake of your children?

# Read and Rise

## Preparing Our Children for a Lifetime of Success

## Introduction

**Congratulations!** You are on your way to making your child a lifelong reader. How? By going about your regular daily activities. Whether you are writing a note to Grandma, reading a bedtime story, or talking about the day's events, you are building a bridge to your child's literacy success.

**Literacy** is more than just being able to read and write. It is the ability to understand and communicate information and ideas by others and to others clearly and to form thoughts using reason and analysis. Literacy is an important tool for later success in life.

### Research Shows:

- The early childhood years, birth to age 4, are critical to literacy development.
- Reading aloud to children appears to be the single most important activity for building the knowledge and skills needed for reading success.
- Children who are exposed to a wide range of words during conversations with adults learn the words they will later need to recognize and understand when reading.
- Studies have shown that, for children whose first language is not English, a strong base in the first language promotes school success in the second language.
- The more children know about reading, writing, listening, and speaking before they arrive at school, the better prepared they are to become successful readers.

**Read on to learn how to use this guide.**

*Read and Rise* author, Kia Brown, is a contributing editor for Scholastic's Early Childhood Division. The Syracuse University graduate has a Masters Degree in Psychological Foundations of Reading from New York University. She is a reading specialist with experience working with struggling and gifted readers.

Resources:
Learning to Read and Write: Developmentally Appropriate Practices for Young Children: A Joint Position Statement by the National Association for the Education of Young Children (NAEYC) and the International Reading Association (IRA). By Susan B. Neuman, Carol Copple, and Sue Bredekamp. (NAEYC, Washington, DC, 2000)

Preventing Reading Difficulties in Young Children by National Research Council. Committee Co-Chairs: Catherine E. Snow and Susan Burns. (National Academy Press, Washington, DC, 1998)

# How to Use This Guide

In this guide, you will find information and ideas that will help you support your child as she grows into a reader.

Young children are eager to learn. To encourage this love of learning, it is important for you to create an environment in your home that provides your child with a number of opportunities to see, hear, and use both oral (spoken) and written language.

The guide is divided by age and grade. Each section includes:

→ An **Introduction**, where you will find brief, research–based information on the common literacy behaviors of the age/grade.

→ A list of **Milestones**—important literacy goals that your child should be able to complete by the end of the age/grade.

→ **Try This!**—ideas and activities that can help you help your child gain the skills needed to become a successful reader.

Please share this guide with your family and friends—it's a wonderful way to get everyone involved in your child's everyday literacy learning. If you are interested in more information on children's books or literacy learning, check out "Your Reading Room" at the end of the guide.

# Contents

## Read and Rise:
### Preparing Our Children for a Lifetime of Success

Written by Kia Brown
Edited by Tom Becker and Karen Proctor
Illustrated by David Kepets

## Infants and Toddlers Birth-2 years

Infants and toddlers thrive on face-to-face interactions—leaning into a crib, cooing and telling a baby how much she is loved, or holding an 18-month-old close and playing a game of "peek-a-boo." This kind of interplay is key to your child's brain development. One of your goals as a parent of an infant or toddler is to surround your child with talk. This exposure happens naturally when you are singing a song or lullaby, reading a story, or just responding to your baby's coos, laughs, and cries.

**The more words a child hears by age 2, the larger her vocabulary will grow. How? Infants and toddlers have neurons (or nerve cells) in the brain for language that are waiting to be wired in. Neuron connections are formed by activity, so the more you talk, the more connections your child has. The more connections your child has, the more vocabulary words she can absorb.**

## Milestones

**Your infant/toddler should:**
- Communicate first with gestures and expressions, then with simple sounds and words.
- Enjoy listening to stories, songs, and rhymes and playing language games.
- Learn to talk and respond to others for the pleasure of interaction.
- Love repetition or hearing the same sounds and stories over and over and over.
- Start using language to explain what she wants, ask questions, and express her feelings and ideas.

## Try This!

- Talk to your child constantly!
- Give simple explanations of what is happening and what will happen next.
- Use a higher pitch and long, drawn-out vowels (for example stretch the "i" in Hi or the "o's" in Good). This helps your baby hear distinct sounds.
- Every day read aloud stories, sing songs or rhymes, and play language games to introduce your baby to the sound of words.
- Create a reading ritual, whether it is before you go to work, after dinner, or at bedtime. Find a comfortable space such as a chair, rug, couch, or bed. Draw your child close to you on your lap. This is key to making reading a lifelong habit.
- Use words she is not familiar with and explain what they mean.

Preschool 3-4 years

Right now your preschooler is busy learning about letters and sounds, pictures and print. You might notice her playing with language by making nonsense sounds and rhyming words, or scribbling on paper. This is great! She is exploring how language and literacy are used in her world. Now is a good time to increase your child's exposure to language and print. You don't have to look far—from the blinking red light that says "Don't Walk" to the label on a cereal box, letters, language, pictures, and print are all around us!

**Reading aloud with your child for just 15 minutes a day will help her become a better reader. Why? When you read with your child, you are showing her how print "works." She is learning how to hold a book, turn pages, listen carefully, and enjoy a story. And she's beginning to understand that print has meaning.**

## Milestones

**Your preschooler should:**
- Enjoy asking a lot of questions and talking about everything.
- Identify labels and signs in her environment.
- Know some letters (such as those in her name) and make some letter-sound matches.
- Understand that print carries a message.
- Enjoy listening to and discussing storybooks, especially her favorite ones, over and over again.

## Try This!

- Talk to your child. Show interest in what he is saying. Play listening games with him that entail verbal clues and directions (for example: I spy with my little eye...).
- Label your child's books, toys, and clothes ("Jackie's shoe"). This will help her identify letters and words, especially her name.
- Read aloud every day, especially from books that reflect your child's culture, home, identity, and language.
- Provide many chances for your child to draw and print using markers, crayons, and pencils. Keep lots of paper (notepads, index cards, envelopes, construction) too!
- Read around your home and community! Help your child read food labels, mail, addresses, messages, and notes. Point out signs, labels and logos in your neighborhood.

## Kindergarten 5-6 years

Your kindergartner will love looking for words, especially familiar ones. She will find them everywhere—from "sale" signs to street signs, from books to buildings. You can help your child make the connection between letters and sounds in fun ways. Try leaving a message to your child on the refrigerator or place a love note in her lunch box. Writing and reading letters and notes will reinforce the power of print in a way that has meaning for your child.

**Write down stories your child tells you. Why? Seeing her own feelings and ideas in print will build her reading confidence. She will also see for herself the different ways print works, such as: words are read from left to right and top to bottom and that words are separated by spaces.**

## Milestones

**Your kindergartner should:**

- Enjoy being read to.
- "Read" familiar books alone, often by memory.
- Use language to explain and explore.
- Write her own name (first and last) and some high-use words (the, mom, dad, and, I, my).
- Know and be able to name uppercase and lowercase letters and make the connections between these letters and the sounds they make.
- Understand that we read English from left to right and top to bottom and be familiar with other concepts of books and print (print has meaning, spaces separate words...).

## Try This!

- Join your local library. (Your child can help fill out her own application!) This is a wonderful way to show how reading and writing are used in everyday life.
  Create a special shelf, one your child can reach, for all the books you borrow from the library.
- Write a story together. Maybe you can start it and your child can fill in the blanks. For example, write, "Once upon a time there was a____. They told their_____ they were going to look for_____." When you're finished, your child can illustrate the story.
- Show your child how people use reading and writing throughout the day. Ask him to help you read and follow a recipe, write a shopping list, and go through the mail with you.
- Have conversations with your child throughout the day. Ask open-ended questions (not yes or no questions) that encourage her to discuss what she's doing, feeling, and thinking.
- Play with letters and sounds. A good start is "Riddle, riddle, ree. I see something you don't see. It starts with the letter B." Let your child guess what you see, then it is her turn to find an object for you to see.

## First Grade 6-7 years

At this very moment, your first grader is learning about the meaning of stories, pictures, words, and language. You might notice your child pointing to each word on the page while she reads aloud. This is great—your child is focusing on letters and the sounds they make. One of your goals as a parent of a first grader is to provide your child with opportunities to read a variety of books and magazines so she can practice her newfound skills. This doesn't have to cost a fortune: Join your local library, participate in your school's book clubs, or share books with neighbors, friends, and relatives.

**Praise your child's reading attempts. Why? When your child makes guesses while reading, she is telling you what she is paying attention to. Saying the word "puppy" for "dog" means that your child is paying attention to the meaning of the story and using clues in the pictures. Saying "dig" for "dog" means that she is paying attention to the letters. Your child is using her own system to figure out what the story means—something that great readers do!**

## Milestones

Your first grader should:
- Read and retell familiar stories in her own words.
- Want to engage in a variety of literacy activities (choosing books she wants to read, writing notes or stories).
- Use letter sounds, sentence meaning, and word parts to identify new words.
- Write about topics that mean something to her.
- Attempt to use some punctuation and capitalization in writing.
- Read aloud books that are on the first grade level with little difficulty.

## Try This!

- Change your reading routine. One day read to your child. And the next day read with your child. Take turns reading each page or character. Then you can listen as your child reads to you. Let older siblings read to your first grader or ask your first grader to read to younger siblings.
- Invite your child to share what she is learning about writing and reading in school. Let your child pick her favorite books and display them around your home.
- Read nonfiction books on topics that interest your child (such as animals, transportation, or history). This will help your child develop the vocabulary she needs to talk about the world around her.
- Help your child write to a relative who lives in a different city. This is a great way not only to practice reading and writing but also to learn about family and heritage.
- Share with your child's teacher examples of what your child can do in writing and reading. Discuss any concerns you may have. Ask how you can continue your child's classroom learning at home.

## Second Grade 7–8 years

Your second grader is becoming more aware of himself as a reader. You might hear your child reading aloud smoothly. Perhaps you can tell from his expressions that he is reading silently for meaning. One of your major goals as a parent of a second grader is to help your child read and write with greater ease and confidence. Praise your child's reading and writing efforts, allow him to pick his own books, correct his errors only when he asks for help, and be understanding if he becomes bored with a book and wants to stop reading it. This will help your second grader become a smarter, more independent reader and writer who is willing to take risks.

**Look at what your child can do! Why? Your child will notice that you are paying attention to her hard work, and that will motivate your child to "improve" and refine her own reading process. If you have any concerns about what your child does not know, share them with her teacher.**

## Milestones

**Your second grader should:**
- Enjoy reading fiction and nonfiction for interest and information.
- Show signs of a growing vocabulary. This includes using language rules when speaking and writing (such as using past and present correctly).
- Have a system that she uses when the meaning of a sentence or paragraph is not clear (such as rereading or questioning).
- Use common letter patterns and letter-sound relationships to spell words.
- Punctuate simple sentences correctly and check her own work for errors.

## Try This!

- Talk to your child about the books he is reading. Ask him to tell you why he likes a certain book or story. Talk about the language, characters, and plot of the story.
- Become involved in school activities and communicate often with your child's teacher. This lets your child know you value education.
- Read for information. Read maps, graphs, charts, and recipes together. Learning how to read a bus schedule is an important life skill.
- Encourage your child to keep a journal. It could be a diary for personal thoughts, a journal in which she writes about books she is reading, or a "dialog journal" the two of you can keep, in which you "talk" to each other by writing notes.
- Let your child see you reading. It doesn't matter if it's a novel, newspaper, or entertainment magazine; it is important that your child discovers that you enjoy reading too.

## Third Grade 8-9 years

Chances are, your child is now reading well on her own. Reading has become a worthwhile and personally rewarding experience. She is reading different types of books—for pleasure. One of your goals as a parent of a third grader is to help your child maintain good reading habits and take responsibility for her own learning. You can do this by simply creating a space in your home where your child can comfortably read and write. Provide a place for books and reference materials such as The Scholastic Children's Dictionary, as well as basic school supplies.

**Continue to read aloud to your child. Why? Children of all ages love to hear stories read aloud. Try more "mature" reading materials—newspapers, magazines, and chapter books, for instance. Reading aloud increases your child's listening comprehension and vocabulary. Ask your child's teacher or your local librarian to suggest books and magazines that are appropriate for your child's age group.**

## Milestones

**Your third grader should:**
- Read longer selections and chapter books independently for enjoyment.
- See connections between different stories.
- Be able to discuss underlying theme or message in fiction and distinguish cause and effect, fact and opinion, main idea and supporting detail in nonfiction.
- Have a rich—and expanding—vocabulary.
- Be attempting different types of writing (such as stories, reports, and poems).
- Make his writing more interesting by adding description and detail.
- Spell more words correctly by seeing how words look and using spelling rules and word parts.

## Try This!

- Never stop talking with your child. Discuss his life in and out of school. Listen, seek solutions together, and soon your child will be sharing his day with you.
- Make writing a habit, an everyday activity. Suggest that your child write her life story. This will give you ideas about what she finds important. Show your approval when your child shares her "special thoughts" with you.
- Stay in regular contact with your child's teacher about his activities and progress in reading and writing.
- Help your child manage her reading life. Together, figure out when to read, study, play, and socialize. Remember: Reading a textbook is also an act of reading.
- Fill your home with books, newspapers, magazines, and other reading materials. When you read, talk about what you think makes for good writing and what makes you like or dislike a particular author's style.

# Reading Room Tips & Resources

## Your Reading Room

Reading at home should feel personal, special, cozy, warm—and fun. We read because it's pleasurable and useful. Read books with your child that she chooses (even if you have read them over and over) and encourage her to read books she likes, independently, even if they seem too easy. Don't feel that what she reads at home has to mirror what she reads at school. Here are some suggestions to get you started.

## Check out these books:

- ***Black Books Galore: Guide to Great African American Children's Books*** by Donna Rand, Toni Parker, and Sheila Foster (John Wiley & Sons, Inc., 1998)
- ***Read to Me: Raising Kids Who Want to Read*** by Bernice E. Cullinan (Scholastic, 1992)
- ***Raising Lifelong Learners: A Parent's Guide*** by Lucy Calkins with Lydia Bellino (Perseus Books, 1997)
- ***Starting Out Right: A Guide to Promoting Children's Reading Success*** The National Research Council, Susan Burns, editor (National Academy Press, 1999)
- ***Straight Talk About Reading: How Parents Can Make a Difference During the Early Years*** by Susan Hall and Louisa Moats (Contemporary Books, 1999)

## Or contact these helpful organizations:

- Scholastic Inc. **http://www.scholastic.com** Scholastic Community Affairs / (212) 343-6100
- National Urban League **http://www.nul.org** Education Department / (212) 558-5300
- Reading Is Fundamental **http://www.rif.org** National Office / (202) 287-3220 or Toll Free (877) RIF-READ
- National Center for Family Literacy **http://www.famlit.org** Family Literacy InfoLine: 1-877-FAMLIT-1
- Reach Out and Read **http://www.reachoutandread.org** National Center / (617) 629-8042
- First Book **http://www.firstbook.org** National Office / (202) 393-1222
- American Library Association **http://www.ala.org** (800) 545-2433
- U.S. Department of Education: Helping Your Child to Learn to Read **http://www.ed.gov**
- The Children's Literature Web Guide **http://www.acs.ucalgary.ca/~dkbrown**
- National PTA **http://www.pta.org**

The National Urban League is the nation's oldest and largest community-based movement devoted to empowering African Americans to enter the economic and social mainstream. Founded in 1910, the heart of the Urban League movement is the professionally staffed Urban League affiliates in more than 100 cities in 34 states and the District of Columbia. The Urban League movement carries out its mission at the local, state, and national levels through direct services, advocacy, research, policy analysis, community mobilization, collaboration, and communications.

The corporate mission of Scholastic Inc., the global children's publishing and media company, is to instill the love of reading and learning for lifelong pleasure in all children. Recognizing that literacy is the cornerstone of a child's intellectual, personal and cultural growth, Scholastic, for more than 80 years, has created quality products and services that educate, entertain and motivate children from pre-K through high school and are designed to help enlarge their understanding of the world around them.

Throughout its history, the company has recognized the importance of working with public, private and nonprofit organizations that share its mission. This commitment to social responsibility is demonstrated today by Scholastic's far-reaching partnerships to address the most critical issues facing children, parents and teachers, with a particular emphasis on reading and literacy. Scholastic Inc. is a proud supporter of the National Urban League's Campaign for African American Achievement.

**National Urban League**
120 Wall Street
New York, NY 10005
Tel (212) 558-5300
Fax (212) 344-5332
www.nul.org

Scholastic Inc.
557 Broadway
New York, NY 10012
Tel (212) 343-6100
Fax (212) 343-4912
www.scholastic.com

# APPENDIX B

## Resource Directory for Parents and Caregivers

The following list includes national organizations involved with educational issues of concern to parents and caregivers. These groups offer a variety of resource material and information about public schools, after-school programs, education technology, and community involvement and advocacy.

**NATIONAL URBAN LEAGUE**
120 Wall Street
New York, NY 10005
212-558-5300
*www.nul.org*

### ADVOCACY ORGANIZATIONS

**Center on Budget and Policy Priorities**
820 1st St., NE
Suite 510
Washington, DC 20002
202-402-1080
*www.cbpp.org*

**Center for Education Reform**
1001 Connecticut Ave., NW
Suite 204
Washington, DC 20036
*www.edreform.com*
800-521-2118

**Center for Law and Social Policy**
1616 P St., NW
Suite 150
Washington, DC 20036
202-328-5140
*www.clasp.org*

**Children's Aid Society**
105 East 22nd St.
New York, NY 10010
212-949-4800
*www.childrensaidsociety.org*

**Children's Defense Fund**
25 E Street, NW
Washington, DC 20001
202-628-8787
*www.childrensdefense.org*

**Civil Rights Project**
Harvard University
124 Mount Auburn Street
Suite 400 South
Cambridge, MA 02138
617-496-6367
*www.law.harvard.edu/civilrights*

**Communities in Schools**
277 Washington St.
Alexandria, VA 22314
800-CIS-4KIDS
*www.cisnet.org*

**Education Trust**
1725 K Street, NW
Suite 204
Washington, DC 20036
800-521-2118
*www.edtrust.org*

**National Association for the Education of Young Children (NAEYC)**
1509 16th Street, NW
Washington, DC 20036
800-424-2460
*www.naeyc.org*

**National Center for Community Education (NCCE)**
1017 Avon Street
Flint, MI 48503
810-238-0463
*www.nccenet.org*

**National Community Education Association (NCEA)**
3929 Old Lee Highway #91-A
Fairfax, VA 22042
703-359-8973
*www.ncea.com*

**Public Education Network**
601 13th St., NW
Suite 900 North
Washington, DC 20005
202-628-7460
*www.publiceducation.org*

**U.S. Charter Schools**
*www.uscharterschools.org*

## AFTER-SCHOOL PROGRAMS

**After-school Alliance**
P.O. Box 65166
Washington, DC 20035
202-296-9378
*www.afterschoolalliance.org*

**Afterschool.gov**
*www.afterschool.gov*

**Center for Youth Development**
Academy for Educational
Development
1825 Connecticut Avenue, NW
Washington, DC 20009
202-884-8000
*www.aed.org*

**National Child Care
Information Center**
Child Care Bureau
Administration for Children
and Families (ACF)
U.S. Department of Health
243 Church, NW, 2nd floor
Vienna, VA 22180
800-616-2242
*www.nccic.org*

**National Institute on Out-of-
School Time**
Wellesley Center for Research
on Women
Wellesley College
106 Central Street
Wellesley, MA 02481

781-283-2547
*www.niost.org*

**21st Century Community
Learning Centers**
U.S. Department of Education
202-219-2164
*www.ed.gov/21stcclc*

## EDUCATIONAL RESOURCES

**Ask ERIC**
*www.askeric.org*

**Big Chalk—The Education
Network**
*www.bigchalk.org*

**Educational Resources
Information Center (ERIC)**
ACCESS ERIC
22777 Research Blvd.
MS 4M
Rockville, MD 20850
800-LET-ERIC
*www.eric.ed.gov/*

**ERIC Clearinghouse on Urban
Education**
Institute for Urban and
Minority Education
Teachers College, Box 40
Columbia University
New York, NY 10027
800-601-4868
*http://eric-web.tc.columbia
.edu/*

**Information Resource Center**
U.S. Department of Education
800-USA-LEARN
*www.ed.gov/index.html*

**National Library of Education**
400 Maryland Avenue, SW
Washington, DC 20202
800-424-1616
*www.ed.gov/NLE/*

**National Parent Information Network (PIN)**
ERIC Clearinghouse on Elementary and Early Childhood Education
University of Illinois at Urbana-Champaign
Children's Research Center
51 Gerty Drive
Champaign, IL 61820
800-583-4135
*www.npin.org*

**The Right Question Project**
2164 Massachusetts Ave.
Suite 314
Cambridge, MA 02140
617-492-1900
*www.rightquestion.org*

## GOVERNMENT ORGANIZATIONS

**Office for Civil Rights**
U.S. Department of Education
Mary E. Switzer Building
330 C Street, SW

Washington, DC 20202
800-421-348l
*www.ed.gov/offices/OCR/*

**U.S. Department of Health and Human Services**
200 Independence Ave., SW
Washington, DC 20201
Toll Free: 877-696-6775
*www.dhhs.gov*

**U.S. Education Department**
400 Maryland Ave., SW
Washington, DC 20202
800-USA-LEARN
*www.ed.gov/*

## LITERACY

**American Library Association**
50 E. Huron
Chicago, IL 60611
800-545-2433
*www.ala.org*

**National Institute for Literacy**
1775 I Street, NW
Suite 730
Washington, DC 20006
202-233-2025
*www.nifl.gov*

## PARENTS' ORGANIZATIONS

**National Parent Teachers Association**
330 N. Wabash Avenue

Suite 2100
Chicago, IL 60611
800-307-4PTA
*www.pta.org*

**Parents for Public Schools**
1520 N. State Street
Jackson, MS 39202
800-880-1222
*www.parents4publicschools.com*

**Partnership for Family
Involvement in Education**
U.S. Department of Education
*http://pfie.ed.gov/*

## TECHNOLOGY

**Black Planet**
*www.blackplanet.com*

**Community Technology
Centers' Network**
*www.ctcnet.org*

**Digital Divide Network**
*www.digitaldividenetwork.org*

**ERIC Clearinghouse on
Information and Technology**
Syracuse University
621 Skytop Rd.
Suite 160
Syracuse, NY 13244
800-464-9107
*www.ericit.org*

## YOUTH ORGANIZATIONS

**Boys & Girls Clubs of America**
800-854-CLUB
*www.bgca.org*

**Camp Fire Boys & Girls**
816-756-1950
*www.campfire.org*

**4-H Council**
301-961-2800
*www.fourhcouncil.edu*

**Girls Inc.**
212-509-2000
*www.girlsinc.org*

**YMCAs of the USA**
312-977-0031
*www.ymca.net*

# REFERENCES

Allen, Walter R. "The Struggle Continues: Race, Equity, and Affirmative Action in U.S. Higher Education." *The State of Black America 2000: Black Americans Under Thirty-Five.* National Urban League, 2001.

Asante, Moleifi Kete. "The Teaching of Black History, K–12." *Urban League Opportunity Journal,* February 1998.

Autman, Samuel. "Charting the College Course." *The San Diego Union-Tribune,* October 23, 2000.

Baker, L., Sher, D., and Mackler, K. "Home and Family Influences on Motivations for Literacy." *Educational Psychologist,* Volume 32, 1997.

Barrett, Paul M. "Baltimore Academy Focuses on Careers." *Wall Street Journal,* May 31, 2001.

Barton, Paul E. and Coley, Richard J. "America's Smallest School: The Family." Policy Information Center, Educational Testing Service, 1992.

Bell-Rose, Stephanie. "African American High Achievers: Developing Talented Leaders." *The State of Black America 2000: Blacks in the New Millennium.* National Urban League, 2000.

Birkett, Frederick A., Ed.M. *Charter Schools: The Parent's Complete Guide.* Prima Publishing, 2000.

Borja, Rhea. "School Efforts in Technology Stalled by Cuts." *Education Week,* November 14, 2001.

Bositis, David A. "School Vouchers Along the Color Line." *The New York Times,* August 15, 2001.

Brown, David W. "Their Characteristic Music: Thoughts on Rap Music and Hip-Hop Culture." *The State of Black America 2000: Black Americans Under Thirty-Five.* National Urban League, 2001.

Brownstein, Ronald. "2 Gloomy Education Reports Should Serve as Guideposts for Reform Effort." *Los Angeles Times,* April 16, 2001.

Bynoe, Yvonne. "The Roots of Rap Music and Hip-Hop Culture: One Perspective." *The State of Black America 2000: Black Americans Under Thirty-Five.* National Urban League, 2001.

Carvin, Andy. "An Inside Look at the New Digital Divide Database." Digital Divide Network, Benton Foundation, 2001.

Christenson, S. L., Rounds, T., and Gorney, D. "Family Factors and Student Achievement." *School Psychology Quarterly,* Volume 7, 1992.

Chubb, John E. "Researchers Probe Achievement Gap." *Education Week,* February 14, 2001.

Clines, Francis X. "Making the Most of a Gift Horse." *The New York Times,* May 24, 2001.

Comer, James P., M.D. *Maggie's American Dream: The Life and Times of a Black Family."* New American Library Books, 1988.

———— *Waiting for a Miracle: Why Schools Can't Solve Our Problems and How We Can.* Dutton, 1997.

Dawson, William. "Youth on the Move: Five High School Teens Forge a Path to the Future." *Urban League Opportunity Journal,* May 2000.

"Dispelling the Myth: High Poverty Schools Exceeding Expectations." The Education Trust, 1999.

Dougherty, Eleanor and Barth, Patte. "How to Close the Achievement Gap." *Education Week,* April 2, 1997.

Dreyfuss, Joel. "Black Americans and the Internet: The Technological Imperative." *The State of Black America 2000: Black Americans Under Thirty-Five.* National Urban League, 2001.

Dubbs, Dana. "Public Education and Careers in the 21st Century." *Urban League Opportunity Journal,* May 2000.

Edelin-Freeman, Kimberly. "African American Men and Women in Higher Education: 'Filling the Glass' in the New Millennium." *The State of Black America 2000: Blacks in the New Millennium.* National Urban League, 2000.

"Falling Through the Net: Defining the Digital Divide." U.S. Department of Education, July 1999.

"Falling Through the Net: Toward Digital Inclusion." U.S. Department of Commerce, October 2000.

Fox, Mem. *Reading Magic: Why Reading Aloud to Our Children Will Change Their Lives Forever.* Harvest Books, 2001.

"From Birth to Fifteen: A Comprehensive Approach to Children's Learning and Development. Reports of Carnegie Corporation of New York, 1989–1996." Includes: *Turning Points: Preparing American Youth for the 21st Century* (1989); *A Matter of Time: Risk and Opportunity in the Nonschool Hours* (1992); *Starting Points: Meeting the Needs of Our Youngest Children* (1994); *Great Transitions: Preparing Adolescents for a New Century* (1995); and *Years of Promise: A Comprehensive Learning Strategy for American Children* (1996). Carnegie Corporation of New York, 1996.

Gest, Ted. "How Five Troubled High Schools Made Dramatic Turnarounds." *U.S. News & World Report,* October 9, 2000.

Gewertz, Catherine. "Research: After the Bell Rings." *Education Week,* February 2, 2000.

Guernsey, Lisa. "Take-Home Test: Adding PC's to Book Bags." *The New York Times,* August 23, 2001.

Hamburg, David A., M.D. *Today's Children: Creating a Future for a Generation in Crisis.* Times Books, 1992.

Haycock, Kati. "Closing the Achievement Gap." *Educational Leadership,* March, 2001.

Hendrie, Caroline. "Student Performance Again Tops List of Concerns." *Education Week,* April 1, 1998.

Herbert, Bob. "Fewer Students, Greater Gains." *The New York Times,* March 12, 2001.

Hess, Frederick M. *Spinning Wheels: The Politics of Urban School Reform.* The Brookings Institution, 1999.

Hetzner, Amy. "Off-Hours Programs Offer a Chance for Fun, to Catch up, Be Safe." *Milwaukee Journal Sentinel,* October 15, 2001.

Heymann, S. Jody and Earle, Alison. "Low-Income Parents: How Do Working Conditions Affect Their Opportunity to Help School-Age Children at Risk?" *American Educational Research Journal,* Winter 2000.

Hoff, David J. "Gap Widens Between Black and White Students on NAEP." *Education Week,* September 6, 2000.

Hrabowski, Freeman A., III, Maton, Kenneth I., and Greif, Geoffrey L. *Beating the Odds: Raising Academically Successful African American Males.* Oxford University Press, 1998.

"It's 3 P.M.—Now What??? Girls Scouts Offer After School Activity Tips." *Kids Source OnLine.* Girl Scouts of the U.S.A., August 17, 1998.

Jacobson, Linda. "New Event Making Case for Better After School Options." *Education Week,* October 11, 2000.

Jencks, Christopher and Phillips, Meredith. "America's Next Achievement Test: Closing the Black-White Test Score Gap." *The American Prospect,* September–October 1998.

Johnston, Robert C. and Debra Viadero. "Unmet Promise: Raising Minority Achievement." *Education Week,* March 15, 2000.

Kozol, Jonathan. *Savage Inequalities: Children in America's Schools.* HarperPerennial Library, 1992.

Lawton, Millicent. "High-Stakes Testing: All-or-Nothing Academics." *Urban League Opportunity Journal,* May 2000.

"Learning to Read and Write: Developmentally Appropriate Practices for Young Children." International Reading Association (IRA) and the National Association for the Education of Young Children (NAEYC). *Young Children,* July 1998.

Lord, Mary. "Founding a Charter School." *U.S. News & World Report,* October 9, 2000.

——— "Making Numbers Make Sense." *U.S. News & World Report,* October 9, 2000.

Manzo, Kathleen Kennedy. "4th Graders Still Lag on Reading Test." *Education Week,* April 11, 2001.

Mathews, Jay. "Study Shows Racial Bias in Special Ed." *Washington Post,* March 2001.

McLaughlin, Milbrey, Irby, Merita A., and Langman, Juliet. *Urban Sanctuaries: Neighborhood Organizations in the Lives and Futures of Inner-City Youth.* Jossey-Bass Publishers, 1994.

McSween, Dachell. "Achievement Matters: The Campaign for African American Achievement." *Urban League Opportunity Journal,* August 1998.

———— "Read and Rise: Guiding African American Children to a Lifetime of Reading." *Urban League Opportunity Journal,* July 2001.

Miller, Doug. "Blacks and the Sciences." *Urban League Opportunity Journal,* May 2000.

"Minority Issues in Special Education." The Civil Rights Project, Harvard University, 2001.

National Center for Education Statistics, U.S. Department of Education. "National Assessment of Educational Progress (NAEP): The Nation's Report Card—Fourth Grade Reading 2000." April 2001.

National Commission on Teaching and America's Future. "What Matters Most: Teaching for America's Future." September 1996.

National Urban League and Scholastic Inc. *Read and Rise: Preparing Our Children for a Lifetime of Success.* Scholastic Inc., 2001.

Newkirk, Thomas. "A Campus Gender Gap." *Education Week,* January 24, 2001.

Novack, Thomas P. and Hoffman, Donna L. "Bridging the Digital Divide: The Impact of Race on Computer Access and Internet Use." *Science,* April 17, 1988.

Patcher, M. *Black-White Contact in Schools: Its Social and Academic Effects.* Purdue University Press, 1982.

Price, Hugh B. *To Be Equal: A Look at Our Nation.* National Urban League, 1999.

Reid, Karla Scoon. "Early Literacy Focus of Urban League Efforts." *Education Week,* December 13, 2000.

Schemo, Diana Jean. "Test Shows Students' Gains in Math Falter by Grade 12." *The New York Times,* August 31, 2001.

Schwartz, Wendy. "A Guide to Choosing an After School Program," *After School Programs for Urban Youth,* Digest No. 114. ERIC Clearinghouse on Urban Education, 2001.

Scott, Katherine Hutt. "Factors Conspire to Keep Poor Students Out of College." *USA Today,* March 5, 2001.

Stafford, Walter W. "The National Urban League Survey: Black America's Under-35 Generation." *The State of Black America 2000: Black Americans Under Thirty-Five.* National Urban League, 2001.

Steinberg, Laurence, Bradford Brown, B., and Dornbusch, Sanford M. *Beyond the Classroom: Why School Reform Has Failed and What Parents Need to Do.* Touchstone Books, 1997.

Stock, Elizabeth. "Computers for Youth: Focusing Digital Divide Efforts on the Home." Digital Divide Network, Benton Foundation, 2001.

Symonds, William C. "How to Fix America's Schools." *BusinessWeek,* March 19, 2001.

Talbott, Emma M. *The Joy and Challenge of Raising African American Children.* Black Belt Press, 1997.

"Technology Counts 2001: The New Divides." *Education Week,* May 10, 2001.

"UF Researcher: After School Activities Help Kids Stay in School." *UF News,* August 31, 2001.

Viadero, Debra. "Even in Well-Off Suburbs, Minority Achievement Lags." *Education Week,* March 15, 2000.

———— "Lags in Minority Achievement Defy Traditional Explanations." *Education Week,* March 22, 2000.

———— "Minority Gaps Smaller in Some Pentagon Schools." *Education Week,* March 29, 2000.

Viadero, Debra and Johnston, Robert C. "Lifting Minority Achievement: Complex Answers." *Education Week,* April 5, 2000.

Ward, Janie Victoria, Ed.D. *The Skin We're In: Teaching Our Children to Be Emotionally Strong, Socially Smart, and Spiritually Connected.* The Free Press, 2000.

Washburn, Gary. "Daley Wants Parents to Help in Kids' Schooling." *Chicago Tribune,* February 15, 2001.

"What Did You Learn in School Today? What Every Student Should Know . . . And Be Able to Do!" Board of Education of the City of New York, 2000–2001 Edition.

Woodward, Emory. "Media in the Home 2000: The Fifth Annual Survey of Parents and Children." Annenberg Public Policy Center of the University of Pennsylvania, 2000.

Zernike, Kate. "Gap Widens Again on Tests Given to Blacks and Whites." *The New York Times,* August 25, 2000.

———— "In 2 Years, Mt. Vernon Test Scores Turn Around." *The New York Times,* May 23, 2001.

Zielbauer, Paul. "In New Haven, a Plan to Make Education Everybody's Business." *The New York Times,* September 2, 2001.

# INDEX